When
Good
Moms
Feel
Bad

When Good Moms Feel Bad

An Empowering Guide for Transforming Guilt, Anxiety, and Anger into Compassion, Confidence, and Connectedness

Jessica Tomich Sorci, LMFT, PMH-C

and **Rebecca Geshuri,** LMFT, PMH-C

balance

NEW YORK BOSTON

Copyright © 2026 by Jessica Tomich Sorci and Rebecca Geshuri

Cover design by Terri Sirma
Cover image © Shutterstock
Cover copyright © 2026 by Hachette Book Group, Inc.

Balance
Hachette Book Group
1290 Avenue of the Americas
New York, NY 10104
GCP-Balance.com
@GCPBalance

First Edition: February 2026

Balance is an imprint of Grand Central Publishing. The Balance name and logo are registered trademarks of Hachette Book Group, Inc.

The publisher is not responsible for websites (or their content) that are not owned by the publisher.

The Hachette Speakers Bureau provides a wide range of authors for speaking events. To find out more, go to hachettespeakersbureau.com or email HachetteSpeakers@hbgusa.com.

Balance books may be purchased in bulk for business, educational, or promotional use. For information, please contact your local bookseller or the Hachette Book Group Special Markets Department at special.markets@hbgusa.com.

Library of Congress Cataloging-in-Publication Data has been applied for.

ISBNs: 9780306837708 (Hardcover); 9780306837722 (Ebook)

Printed in Canada

MRQ-T

10 9 8 7 6 5 4 3 2 1

Contents

Introduction

You're Normal—Angry Parts and All

Motherhood is dangerous to mental health. Mothers reporting poor or fair mental health surged 64 percent between 2016 and 2023, marking a significant decline in maternal well-being nationwide.[1] For new moms, the statistics are even more concerning: One in five receives a maternal mental health diagnosis,[2] and suicide is a primary cause of death during the first year postpartum.[3] Given the stigma surrounding maternal mental health and systemic barriers to treatment, these statistics likely underrepresent the magnitude of the actual crisis. It's clear that moms desperately need better access to mental health support.

Though we are collectively reliant on mothers for the health and well-being of our entire species, moms are neglected and largely forgotten in their vulnerable years. Our society places enormous burdens of responsibility on mothers, implores them to be anxious about each and every risk involved with pregnancy and parenthood, and then leaves them to figure it out, alone. America is generally unsupportive, disempowering, unrewarding, and shaming to mothers as they make their way through the most tender times of their (and their children's) lives.

The messaging moms receive is this: If you're unhappy with motherhood, it's not because you're getting shortchanged by society—it's because you're a bad mom. Something's wrong with you. Good moms love motherhood! Period. When a woman becomes a mother, the people around her collectively focus on the belly, the baby, and all the accompanying consumerism, and of course, a little later, there's the push to get Mom back to her pre-baby body and sex life and work performance. But no one asks about you, the mom. No one considers the fact that this is an INCREDIBLY HARD TIME for you—and it is! No one inquires lovingly about your despair or your anxiety. They smile and coo at your baby and ask if baby is sleeping through the night yet. And you—being the good mom that you are—feel like a failure because no, your baby hasn't EVER slept more than a three-hour stretch, so clearly, you're doing something wrong. You must be a bad mom because you don't feel cheerful, you dread nights and mornings and afternoons alike, your baby cries all the time, and you're too afraid to admit it, but you're starting to think this was all a huge mistake. You're the one ginormous dark spot obscuring the rainbow that was supposed to be motherhood.

We've all bought into the false belief that only *bad* moms have enraged parts, unfulfilled parts, parts that want to go back in time to when there were no children. Only bad moms have parts that sometimes feel like calling the whole effing thing off. We harbor what we think is a dark little secret: that we're having a very hard time, not loving the journey, behaving badly, making the wrong decisions, and feeling unfulfilled. Outwardly, we focus almost exclusively on doing a good job of trying to stave off the negative self-talk that's looping 24/7 inside of us. We try hard to be good moms by exiling all the thoughts and feelings we have deemed to be bad. We try *so hard*, in fact, we burn ourselves out and become resentful, fried little versions of who we once were.

When being *you* conflicts with being a *good mom*, war breaks out inside. Part of you becomes explosive with rage, while another part of you becomes masterful at hiding it. Part of you is full of self-hatred, and another part works hard to be more disciplined. Part of you bites back words and wishes and longing, while another part surreptitiously tries to find some soothing to fill the void wherever you can, bingeing on ice cream, alcohol, screen time, self-harm, or some other state-inducing intoxicant that's accessible and is yours and yours alone.

A Paradigm Shift

We affectionately call parts specific to motherhood "Mom Parts." Your Mom Parts show up to manage and cope with the transformation, responsibilities, and losses you experience on your motherhood journey. Parts can create symptoms that begin to pile up and cluster together over the months and years. Those clusters form into familiar constellations that we commonly call Rage, Depression, and Anxiety. It's very easy for moms to qualify for mental health diagnoses (insert sad face here). Diagnoses fail to include the impact of crappy social support and are pathologizing in their identification of moms as the source of unwellness. And yet, diagnoses are sometimes helpful and necessary. In our patriarchal system with its emphasis on hyper-productivity and individualism and its accompanying dearth of social services, a diagnosis can help a mom obtain care and support to which she may not otherwise have access.

And...we don't know of any moms who don't wade through the deep waters of shame, fear, and loss. Many of us get caught in the current and swept away by the magnitude of our inner torment. Some of us are pulled under, into the dark and empty silence of our emotional turbulence. Is this mental illness? Or is this motherhood? Either way, moms have parts that are in serious pain, and those parts need attention and care.

If you're anything like the rest of us, you were probably never taught to be curious about your inner world. Did anyone show you or tell you how to direct compassion toward your own suffering? Most of us were taught to try to get rid of "bad" feelings. As a girl and as a woman and mother, you were probably taught that it's selfish to focus on yourself. You were born to nurture and accommodate everyone else, right? Good moms sacrifice a lot, and they (try to) like it. They smile through it, and they stay patient and generous. Only...

Even good moms have a breaking point. Even good moms have needs and limitations. Even good moms have nervous systems that respond and react. And those nervous systems deserve the best care. We're giving you a model for better understanding yourself, so that you become empowered to help yourself feel better in direct and immediate ways. While there is a shit ton that is outside of your control in momlife, there are some key areas where you do have the power to make a dramatic impact on your own well-being. The key to feeling better starts with befriending your *parts*.

The IFS Revolution

Internal Family Systems is a relatively young model of psychotherapy that's providing millions of people a new way to feel greater self-acceptance and inner calm. IFS is an evidence-based parts model that revolves around the idea that we as humans have many different subpersonalities existing simultaneously within us. All of our parts need to be known and related to respectfully, the same way all people need to be known and related to respectfully. Moms feel relieved when they discover that all their parts (even the ones that scare them) make sense and have wisdom.

IFS believes that everything about you makes sense and has wisdom, even the funky stuff. By assuming that all people contain multitudes of parts, we can approach any feeling or behavior with interest rather than with judgment or fear. Our parts emerge out of necessity in critical moments to ensure our belonging and survival, imprinting deeply into our identities, frozen at the age when they formed. Consequently, they're usually quite young. Like all little kids, our parts lack maturity, finesse, and perspective. They're here to do a particular job because at some point in time, your nervous system determined it was absolutely necessary.

Some of our parts get a bad rap and are disliked by us or by the people around us. But as we look closer at the parts of us we refer to as anxiety, depression, or anger, we come to find out that those parts are here trying to help us. They each have their own hopes and fears. They aren't just symptoms to be eradicated but are, in fact, heroic, hardworking parts that deserve appreciation and care. By seeing them in this welcoming light, we set the stage for a brand-new way of relating to the parts of us that cause the most trouble and hold the most pain.

HOW INTERNAL FAMILY SYSTEMS LOOKS AT PARTS

ALL parts are welcome.

ALL parts have good intentions.

Parts are stuck in the past.

Healing means separating (unblending) from our parts and caring for them.

IFS is about turning *toward* our parts and beginning to develop relationships with them. Understanding and validating our parts (even the ones that are very disliked inside us and outside us) is called *befriending*. Befriending our parts is the beginning of helping them soften, relax, and yield to more desirable roles within our systems. This goes against nearly every standard psychotherapeutic model that strives to reduce and remove unwanted symptoms or sees the inner world in terms of behaviors to get rid of and problems to overcome. In IFS, all parts are not only welcome but vital. All parts need to be respected and heard—just like all children need to be respected and heard.

When we are hurt or traumatized, especially in childhood, some of our parts adapt to help us survive whatever horrible thing is happening, and those parts inadvertently take on burdens and false beliefs. Those burdens and false beliefs generally stick with us throughout our lives, unless we have an opportunity (like you do today) to turn toward them and bring them into the light of caring awareness. In adulthood, we find that many of our parts are outdated, still believing narratives from our childhood experiences that no longer hold true today. We have a chance now to update those parts and release them into more desirable functioning within our systems.

There are two categories of parts: protectors and exiles. Protectors are further divided into managers and firefighters. Managers are protector parts that run our day-to-day lives and try to keep our painful vulnerability far, far away. They stay in control by being proactive, people-pleasing, and hardworking. These are the parts that strive for improvement and growth—the polished versions we present to other moms, neighbors, and coworkers. They do most of the mothering tasks and band together to direct resources to our kids. In our mom lingo, we call these parts Good Mom parts.

Firefighters are also protector parts—but they're the ones that react when we feel exposed or threatened. They try to extinguish our overwhelming feelings and distance us from our pain, often in extreme or destructive ways. They don't try to proactively ward off pain—rather, they jump in reactively, after the flames have already started burning (hence the name *firefighters*). They have the same goal as managers (to help us), but their strategies are more impulsive and extreme. These are often the parts we pretend we don't have. They're our Bad Mom parts, and they show up when we hit our breaking point.

Exiles are young, vulnerable parts that have experienced trauma and are isolated from the rest of the system. They carry memories, sensations, and emotions from formative events and remain stuck in the past. The core wound in nearly all our exiles is the belief that we are not good enough, not lovable, or not worthy. The concept of "exiles" encompasses a wide range of trauma that can be difficult to access, especially for moms who are harried and sleep-deprived. To provide greater accessibility and efficiency for mothers, we created the concept of the Inner Baby, to convey the tenderness and sensitivity of these young parts in a simple, inviting way. Inner Baby parts include Sad, Scared, and Wanting parts. Because of their tenderness, they easily absorb burdens of shame, fear, helplessness, despair, worthlessness, sorrow, fragility, and emptiness. Their pain is the reason our protectors jump into action.

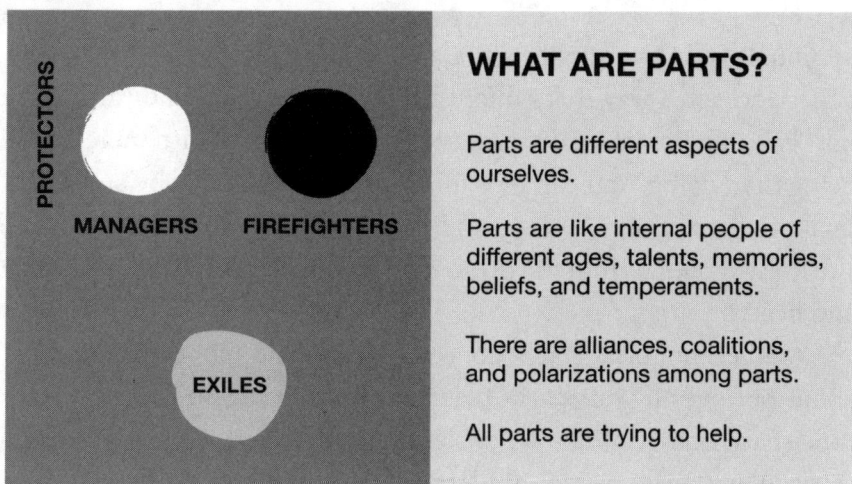

PROTECTORS

MANAGERS   FIREFIGHTERS

EXILES

WHAT ARE PARTS?

Parts are different aspects of ourselves.

Parts are like internal people of different ages, talents, memories, beliefs, and temperaments.

There are alliances, coalitions, and polarizations among parts.

All parts are trying to help.

Parts have hopes and fears that inform their functioning. Asking the simple question *What is this part hoping for or afraid of?* yields a wealth of information about what function it's attempting to serve and what it really needs.

Self (with a capital *S*) is who we are when our parts aren't "up." Self has the qualities of a capable, caring mother who is in a healthy, supportive relationship with less-developed, more wounded, or frightened aspects of our beings (i.e., parts). We call Self the Inner Mom.

Inner Mom

- Curiosity
- Compassion
- Calmness
- Clarity
- Confidence
- Connectedness
- Courage
- Creativity
- Choice

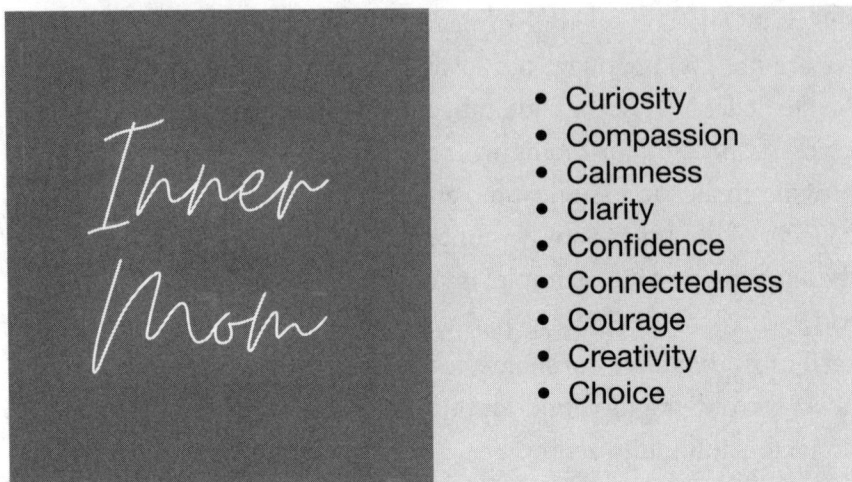

Our Inner Mom gives us the ability to be present with our past experiences in a way that's interested, open, attentive, and caring. It's not "calming down" or disregarding/squashing parts. It's more about being than doing. You can recognize Inner Mom energy by any of the qualities listed above, but we find that curiosity is the easiest way in. Curiosity moves us into the present moment and opens our eyes, ears, and hearts.

Another important IFS concept is unblending. Unblending is about peeling off your part's perspective just a bit, so that you get a little space from it. When we're blended with a part, we're activated or dysregulated (e.g., pissed off, despairing, or freaked out), and we see the situation in very black-and-white terms. We don't feel spacious; we feel swallowed by emotion and engulfed in sensation. Learning how to unblend introduces a massively powerful new tool into our maternal tool kit. (See Blending/Unblending box, opposite.)

The last big IFS concept we want to prep you with is this one: Parts get polarized. It's pretty wild how much distress our own parts can create inside of us when they oppose each other. Moms have Good Mom and Bad Mom parts battling inside of them every day, fighting hard against each other for what they need and for what they

BLENDING	UNBLENDING
Experiencing parts as Self ("I'm so mad!")	Recognizing parts as parts ("Part of me is really angry.")
Dysregulated	Regulated
Operating from protection	Operating from connection
Past flooding the present	Past distinct from the present
Black-and-white thinking	Seeing multiple perspectives
Reactive	Responsive

believe in. Understanding this concept is super helpful for interrupting destructive, heartbreaking relational patterns and dynamics that have a tendency to follow us through the years. Developing the ability to moderate between our polarized parts brings new peace and calm into our nervous systems.

POLARIZATIONS

- Conflict between two protector parts.

- Each side is afraid of and opposed to the other's agenda.

- Each protects vulnerability (sometimes the same vulnerability).

Getting to know your Mom Parts gives you an empowering and transformative way to bring more peace into your inner world. Learning how to relate to your Good Mom parts and your Bad Mom parts gives you a path to becoming friendlier with everything that shows up in you. Mapping how your parts show up can help you start to anticipate them, disarm them, and effectively *mother them* in the manner they've been needing for a very long time. This book is here to provide a new way of understanding your internal system so that there's space for you and your child to coexist more harmoniously in your psychology—even when the two of you are in conflict. You don't have to choose between being selfish or selfless. You can stop putting so much energy into NOT feeling disappointed, sad, or angry as a mom.

Mothering is the heart of our humanity. Moms are forming and influencing our next generation of leaders, and there is no more important job on this planet. Helping moms thrive translates into improved health for our world. As long as our culture continues to fail at truly valuing mothering, moms are going to continue to show up as "disordered," and the statistics will continue to reflect an unhappy, unhealthy population. Moms need help.

Helping Moms from the Inside

Good mental health is not the absence of symptoms, struggle, or suffering. If you're here on planet Earth, you're going to get your share of all that. This book won't provide a cure for your distress, but it will introduce you to new ways of understanding yourself. As you learn how to go inside your inner world and greet your parts, you'll get to know yourself intimately, the same way you got to know your baby when they were new to you, and the same way you got to know your child as they developed new capacities and inclinations. The better you know and understand yourself, the better you can support and care for yourself.

Good moms feel bad when they aren't getting the care they need from outside. They also feel bad when they aren't getting the care they need from inside. There is a growing advocacy movement that's working hard to address the significant external systemic problems that moms and families face. Thank God. Change and improvement can't come swiftly enough. We are so grateful for the courageous advocates who are working tirelessly to increase public awareness and upgrade public policy. This book will spend very little time belaboring our considerable external policy and systemic problems.

Who We Are and Our Discovery

As psychotherapists, our credentials and expertise don't equip us to tackle these massive external systemic problems. But as experts in maternal mental health and Internal Family Systems, we are equipped to help with the inner suffering that moms experience. We are the advocacy movement for internal care. We've written these words with the goal of directly helping you get immediate relief today, despite the state of the world around you. We're going to teach you a way to infuse your internal world with self-compassion, so that regardless of external circumstances, things feel better inside of you.

For the past fifteen years, our psychotherapy practices have been exclusively focused on treating mothers in distress. As Internal Family Systems certified therapists who are also certified in perinatal mental health, we began to recognize that we hold a unique skill set that enables us to identify and speak to the pain that moms are feeling and help them get out from under the shame and stigma that come with being an unhappy, "failing" mom. As moms ourselves, we are well acquainted with our own Mom Parts and have lived through many of the painful experiences our clients bring to us. We know how it feels to be undersupported while mothering and simultaneously experiencing an internal-parts battle. And we also know how it feels to *unblend* from those battling parts and get some hugely relieving breathing room.

We first learned about unblending in 2018 when we attended a workshop in Santa Cruz where Richard Schwartz introduced a small group of therapists to his parts model and effectively blew our minds. What we learned that day changed us personally and professionally.

In our consultation hours, we took to using Post-it notes to track and organize the parts that were showing up in ourselves and in our clients. Yellow and pink squares cluttered the walls, filling them with words like "angry," "scared," "resentful," helping trace and track the internal experiences of moms, creating clearer narratives that led more directly to the source of their pain. We were liberated and inspired as we brought the good news back to the moms in our practices: "Of course you have a Resentful part! You've been up all night feeling scared and sad with a sick kid! You're still a good mom!"

And something really remarkable happened to our clients: By seeing themselves as composed of all kinds of parts and then naming those parts and speaking on behalf of those parts, moms started making more sense to themselves. They started to feel more compassion and understanding for the loads they were carrying, and for the fact that they reached their breaking point and lost their shit sometimes. They felt new permission to call their suffering what it is—grief and shame. The omnipresent mom shame started sliding off, and people were arriving at transformative truths much more quickly. They started sharing more honestly with other moms and discovering new solidarity and connection.

Our idea for *When Good Moms Feel Bad* began to take shape as a way to help mothers improve their mental health with or without a therapist, on their own or within a group. Over the past several years, we have continued to expand our Mom Parts methodology beyond the therapy room and into a comprehensive curriculum for healthcare practitioners who are wildly excited about implementing this unique interpretation of IFS with their mom clients. Because it helps. So. Much.

This Book Is for ALL Moms

Moms at all stages of mothering are teeming with symptoms of anxiety and depression, guilt, overwhelm, and rage. They're harsh and ruthlessly unforgiving of themselves. In our many years of working with moms, we've discovered recurring themes that can't be ignored. We have found ourselves naming the same kinds of Mom Parts again and again, even with clients from wildly different backgrounds and of different ethnicities and disparate ages. So much about the maternal experience cuts across racial, socioeconomic, and cultural lines.

Wherever you are on your mom journey, and no matter how you came to be a mom or a stepmom or an adoptive mom or a foster mom, or a mom of a child who died, or a grandma—however your kids and your motherhood happened—all moms begin as new moms. And in our newness, we are all so vulnerable and shaky and unsure and stretched thin. Our time as new moms imprints us as mothers. How we see ourselves in those early months and years is the root of what grows into our burgeoning identity as humans and as mothers.

New moms are like sponges, soaking up care and love to whatever extent it's available. We're depleted and we need nourishment and tending. Matrescence is a term coined by anthropologist Dana Raphael to describe the developmental phase of life that moms experience when they become mothers.[4] Like all significant human developmental phases, matrescence includes wild physiological transformation (hello, hormones; hi, brain changes!), as well as social changes (why is it that everyone always says hi to my baby and not to me anymore?) and spiritual changes (what used to feel important suddenly feels trivial—who am I now?).

Did you get what you needed as a new mom? If not, how did you make it through? Your answer to this question will start to highlight which parts of you came forward in response to your unmet needs. Whether you identify as a new mom or a mom formerly known as a new mom, working with your parts will give you incredible tools and access to more self-compassion. Reflecting on your early days as a mom is a tender and meaningful endeavor that will help lead you to greater understanding of yourself and your Mom Parts.

This book isn't just for good moms who feel bad. It's also for "bad" moms who feel bad. Some moms may self-describe as bad, or secretly battle shameful beliefs about their badness, based on histories of having been abusive or addicted or negligent or absent. This book is for you too. It will be a brand-new concept for you to imagine that the parts of you who identify as *bad* are being invited in. And those unwanted parts can be helped so dramatically by a shift in perspective.

Mothering isn't something only cisgender women do. "Mothering" is a verb, and anyone who cares for and bonds with a dependent baby or child from a position of responsibility is in some way mothering that child. If the word "mom" feels exclusive to you, we want to open our arms right here and welcome you back in. This idea that you have parts particular to caring for a dependent person whom you are raising means you're having a unique experience that is both shaping you and opening you up in vulnerable ways. You require and deserve extra care. This book was created to support you in the vital work you do. For anyone who is *mothering* a child, we appreciate you and welcome you here. If it's helpful, feel free to sub in a word other than "mom" that works better for you (parent, dad, caregiver, etc.).

This is your chance. This book is for you. It's designed to help you understand, respect, and trust yourself, even if you think the damage has already been done or the past is far behind you. Moms of mature adults still get emotional when they reflect back on their birth stories, regardless of the decades that have passed. The memories live on in your parts, and your parts can be healed with care and attention. It takes courage to open your heart to the injuries and wounds you tucked out of sight. You can go slowly. Know that you aren't alone.

How to Use This Book

Our hope in creating this body of work is that it will help you get acquainted with the concept of "parts" so that you start to take an interest in the good intentions of all your reactivity, on a path to better understanding and appreciating yourself. Throughout the book, you will find the following guides:

- JOURNAL—this is a prompt to grab your journal and start writing. Answering and exploring these questions will help you form your own narrative about motherhood. Understanding the story of your Mom Parts helps you know why they feel and act the way they do. Understanding yourself is a major key to empowerment and to feeling better. We recommend having a dedicated Mom Parts journal.
- ✳—these are kernels of wisdom. We've distilled some of our central, most important and useful ideas down into pithy take-aways. These ✳ are highlights, meant to help you get what you need on your path to understanding and trusting yourself as a mom.
- Stories about moms—throughout the book, we weave in stories from moms we've worked with who benefited from getting to know their Mom Parts. Note that names and identifying details have been changed for privacy and that some stories are com-pilations. That said, know that these struggles and insights are tender and real and by sharing them, we hope to communicate loudly that you are not alone! You make sense.

Part 1 of the book lays out concepts and explanations that will help you gain curiosity about and compassion for the experience you've had as a mom so far, softening assumptions you've carried about selflessness and selfishness. We lean into the belief that good mental health is not about the absence of pain; good mental health is more about the quality of the relationship you have with yourself. To help you build a better relationship with yourself, in part 1 we intro-duce you to Internal Family Systems and offer a complete guide to your Mom Parts, inviting you to explore and build relationships with your parts. Listening to your parts and getting to know them well helps you understand how they function and gives you new insights into disrupting repetitive loops.

Part 2 is about healing. Healing begins the moment you recognize that you have parts and that your parts are trying to help you. This kind of healing is an ongoing, lifelong process. You will likely feel some immediate relief just by identifying your parts, but like children, our parts need ongoing tending. Part 2 teaches you how to explore and care for your Mom Parts.

At the end of the book, you will find nudges, reminders, and exercises to help you along. You can experiment with the exercises on your own or with someone you trust—a therapist is great, and close friends or a mom's group can work well too. Have some paper and a pen available so you can keep track of your findings as you go— a dedicated journal would be even better. We've spent many hours with moms individually and in community groups using these tools, and time and again, we've been amazed by the depth of healing that moms have reported.

A friendly word of caution: Doing this internal work alone isn't a great idea for moms who have severe trauma histories that have not been explored in therapy. This book is designed to support you in identifying and befriending your protector parts, but it's not a substitute for IFS therapy, which has the power to guide you into healing your deepest wounds and most painful beliefs. Parts work can stir up exiled material that deserves and requires the care of a skilled clinician or experienced healer. If you have a significant trauma history, please don't stop reading—but please do reach out to someone who can adeptly support you on your journey. (Here is a link to the IFS practitioner directory: https://ifs-institute.com/practitioners.)

Practitioners of IFS like to say, "We go slow to go fast." Slowing down to notice what's going on inside you may feel counterintuitive or like a chore. But if you have a little spare courage in your reservoir, let's just experiment. We're in this together. Good moms and bad moms. Ready to give it a try?

PART ONE

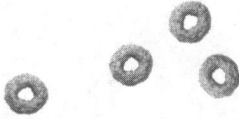

Selfless or Selfish?

Chapter 1

Good Moms Feel the Worst

We're pretty sure you're a good mom. You're motivated to raise happy, healthy children. You want to be some combination of comforting, supportive, encouraging, and helpful to your kids. You put an enormous amount of effort and thought into mothering, and you show up day after day, with determination and love. You care and you try. You take feedback seriously and you grow. That sounds like a formula for winning and like a description of good mothering to us, and yet so many moms who fit that description feel bad. You feel bad about yelling or you feel bad about your kids' (lack of) development, or you feel bad about feeling depressed or feeling as anxious as you do. You feel bad about your body, bad about the state and condition of your partnership, or bad about how you're longing for more than you have. You feel bad about your performance at work or bad about the fact that you're a stay-at-home mom or bad that you don't spend enough time with your kids. You feel bad about the way you hound them, but also about how little impact you seem to have on them. Most of the moms we know use words like "failure," "guilt," and "not good enough" when they describe themselves. Even though they look like good moms, and their kids love them, and they put in a ton of good-mom hours, they feel awful much of the time.

Early motherhood is an enormous life overhaul for all of us, rendering us breathless and humbled at best, terrified and despairing in our darker moments. To become a mom in the context of America's perfectionistic, individualistic, patriarchal culture that fails abysmally at providing care and support to mothers means contending with our Mom Parts all alone. We want to be good moms and yet sometimes we feel pretty fucking terrible as we fight through sleep deprivation, the awkwardness of a new role, and trying to soothe a crying baby who needs us 24/7. We have parts that are obsessed with the baby's safety. We have parts that hate motherhood. We're shocked by our own visceral unhappiness as well as our longing to be close to the baby, whom we feel completely addicted to. New motherhood, or matrescence, is a confusing, disorienting developmental phase of life. It's a formative time when we are growing our identity as moms. Oh, and additionally, we are assigned the job of being the first teachers and the primary shapers of our children's long-standing health and future wellness. (No pressure.)

JOURNAL

Thinking back to the early days, even if it was long, long ago, what do you remember about that time? Close your eyes and recall that younger version of you. Picture her—the hardworking, tired new mom who was brand-new to the experience of motherhood.

Do you remember how you felt in your body?

What kind of thoughts and beliefs did you start to form about yourself as a mother?

What were some of the feelings that came up toward your child?

Who was there to help you?

What messages did you receive from the people around you?

What ideas did you bring into motherhood from your own childhood?

Write down any thoughts, feelings, or memories that help give shape to the new-mom version of you. Remembering your beginning is the start of honoring yourself as a mom. We're sure it hasn't been easy for you. And we know you've never told the whole story of how you got here. You likely haven't felt listened to and understood—at least not completely. Let your parts know you're listening now.

When Motherhood Meets America

In today's society, a collective agreement has emerged about you as a mother: If you're having a hard time, it's because there's something wrong with you. You have a chemical imbalance/your hormones are off, you have a psychological disorder, or perhaps, more ominously, it's that you're just not a good mom. You have a character problem, you're selfish or uneducated or lacking in . . . something really vital for good momming. This cultural trance and the distorted perception it creates are the cause for much suffering in motherhood.

In fact, motherhood is difficult for two reasons: because it transforms a person's entire physical and psychological being, rendering that person immensely vulnerable; AND because the world fails to notice or care. (Also, it's a ton of work. Okay, so maybe three reasons.) It is absolutely true that moms do not get the care or support that's needed to sustain them while they do the labor and nervous-system hosting that are required to meet the needs of babies and children. Moms are expected to give of themselves freely, completely, and abundantly, with no breaks and without themselves breaking. There is virtually no social support in the US for mothers, and despite the fact that there is inadequate healthcare, no national paid family leave, almost nothing in the form of postpartum respite provided, a lack of workplace flexibility, and very little safe and affordable childcare, moms are expected to be happy while simultaneously holding responsibility for mothering really, really well.

The external pressure to be a good mom is larger than life, and we don't skimp on the harsh internal criticism or mom-related self-loathing either. Opportunities to feel like we're not measuring up or we're outright failing abound. While it's postpartum depression that grabs headlines, our maternal mental health crisis in the United States extends all the way down the long road to grandmotherhood and generously includes adoptive moms, foster moms, queer moms, and stepmoms. Motherhood and its pain points change over time, but it never stops upending us. Moms are in distress, and we need help. The surgeon general issued an advisory statement in 2024 highlighting the urgent need for America to better support parents. He connected the dots between parental distress and unwell children, calling for "a fundamental shift in how we value and prioritize the mental health and well-being of parents."[1] Maybe the powers that be are finally beginning to catch on. Until the world around us responds appropriately to the needs of mothers, moms will go on suffering under the illusion that we are the ones falling short.

Beyond Black-and-White

To be clear, there is no such thing as a good mom or a bad mom. Good and bad are binary constructs that are too absolute to capture the subtle, nuanced reality of motherhood. Good and bad can't begin to describe the tangled jungle of emotion that's alive in the relational landscape of mother and child. Good and bad provide only a black-and-white duality and are the most base and simplistic way we can describe something. As small children, we began using those words along with "mean" and "nice" to differentiate what was acceptable from what was unacceptable, and in direct response to how our parents or our culture wanted us to behave. Don't be bad—be good. Don't be mean—be nice. As sophisticated and insightful as we may become in adulthood, we never quite shake the fear of being bad and the aspiration to be good. In times of stress or threat, we quickly revert back to our most basic and undeveloped selves, splitting the world and ourselves into good and bad. That keeps things simple and gives us a clear objective around which to operate: Get rid of what's bad and just be good.

Good and bad, in their black-and-whiteness, aren't adequate descriptions of people—certainly not of moms. These overly simple words are powerful descriptions of judgments we've made about *parts* of ourselves—parts that behave in certain ways, that have particular thoughts and feelings, and that have desires. The world outside echoes our internalized ideas of good and bad too; certain kinds of actions, feelings, thoughts, and desires are a yes or a no—and all of us get the memo. We polarize, with an intense energy on either side, opposite and equal in its extremeness. When we're bad, we try harder to be good. And when we're good, we do what it takes to keep being good, often labeling other moms as bad. For those of us who are over-achievers, we start eyeing "perfect" and wondering if we can get ourselves over there, into perfection, out of the polarized tension of good and bad. Perfection sells itself as the safest destination of all, where we will be out of the line of fire, never to be mistaken for a bad person or, worse, a bad mom.

Ideas of good and bad and perfect don't help moms decrease their stress, restore their integrity, or heal. Good and bad create a feedback loop that perpetuates the same feelings, thoughts, and actions that are generating our unhappiness. To break out of the loop of striving to be a selfless, good mom and coming up short and feeling like a selfish, bad mom—and then doubling down with superstriving—we need to look more closely at what it is we're calling good and bad.

It turns out we have *parts* of ourselves that self-describe as good and create outwardly likable or acceptable personas that other people agree are good. And we also have parts of us that our systems judge as bad, that are full of panic, hate, terror, and anger, usually left over from childhood when we were powerless and subjected to poor treatment by others. It's really not good moms and bad moms we're talking about here. We're talking about parts of us that cast judgment about goodness and badness. We have parts that deeply and fundamentally mistrust us—that have come to believe through early experience that we are, in fact, bad. Certain of those parts take on leadership roles inside of us in stressful times. And motherhood is a very stressful time.

What Are These *Parts* That We Speak Of?

The term "parts" is integral to Internal Family Systems (IFS), an evidence-based model of psychotherapy that has completely changed the way we understand human beings, helping shed new light on the internal dynamics of mothers in our psychotherapy practices. IFS has been demonstrated to be effective with some of the most hard-to-treat mental health disorders, including OCD, addiction, and dissociative identity disorder, in that it assumes that all people have many "parts" of themselves that compose the whole of their psychology. By addressing people as not just one singular personality, but as naturally having multiple parts structured around an indestructible core Self, IFS brings us exciting insights and options for healing. In his book *No Bad Parts*, Richard Schwartz, the creator of IFS, tells us that parts are "little inner beings who are trying their best to keep you safe."[2] To ensure you're protected, some parts take on roles that other parts are completely opposed to. Within one individual, teams of parts form, composed of parts who share common goals and complementary strategies for advancing your survival and safety or increasing your inclusion and belonging.

Parts usually take shape early in life, adaptively supporting who and how we need to be to exist in our families of origin. Our parts form in precisely the best way to keep us safe and connected in our primary attachment relationships (i.e., mom and dad and siblings). Those parts and their beliefs and behaviors tend to persist, even when they are no longer adaptive or conducive to our health. Moving through the world with childlike, outdated parts becomes a bit problematic for us as adults. Parents commonly find themselves acting like children with their own children, feeling just as powerless and panicky as they did when they were small. IFS gives us a formula for changing our reactive patterns. We can turn toward our angry, panicky parts with curiosity and uncover their childlike hopes and fears. Listening to those kid-like parts and then recognizing that we're able to approach triggering moments with adult resources grows us up and starts to heal our childhood wounds.

In IFS, parts are divided into two categories: exiles and protectors. There are two types of protectors: managers and firefighters. Exiles are the sensitive parts of us that have been wounded, and protectors are the parts of us that emerge to guard and protect those wounded parts. In this book, we mostly focus on protectors, as they are the Mom Parts that do all the heavy lifting and the parts that moms are most in contact with. Sometimes the healing and unburdening of exiles happens spontaneously and organically as you begin to bring more self-compassion into your system. Mom Parts point to the vulnerability of exiles that exist within our "Inner Baby," homing in on Sad, Scared, and Wanting parts as the most familiar and common (über-vulnerable) parts that hold fear, shame, and grief. Focusing on getting to know our protectors has the powerful effect of unlocking our vulnerability and helping us develop new capacities. As our internal family of parts begins to relax, we are granted access to a restorative internal energy that IFS calls "Self." Your Self is different from your parts. Self has an innate kind of vitality and wellness that cannot be destroyed (no matter what!). Everyone has a Self, regardless of the traumas you've endured or the bad things you've done.

Here's an image adapted from IFS, which we've adjusted to include our Mom Parts terminology. This image helps make clear how Self, aka the Inner Mom, is at the center of our internal system, and all our parts weave in and around her.

IFS is a constraint/release model, which means the moment our protectors (Good Mom parts and Bad Mom parts) relax (even just a little), BOOM—Self is there. Relaxed protectors open up more spacious

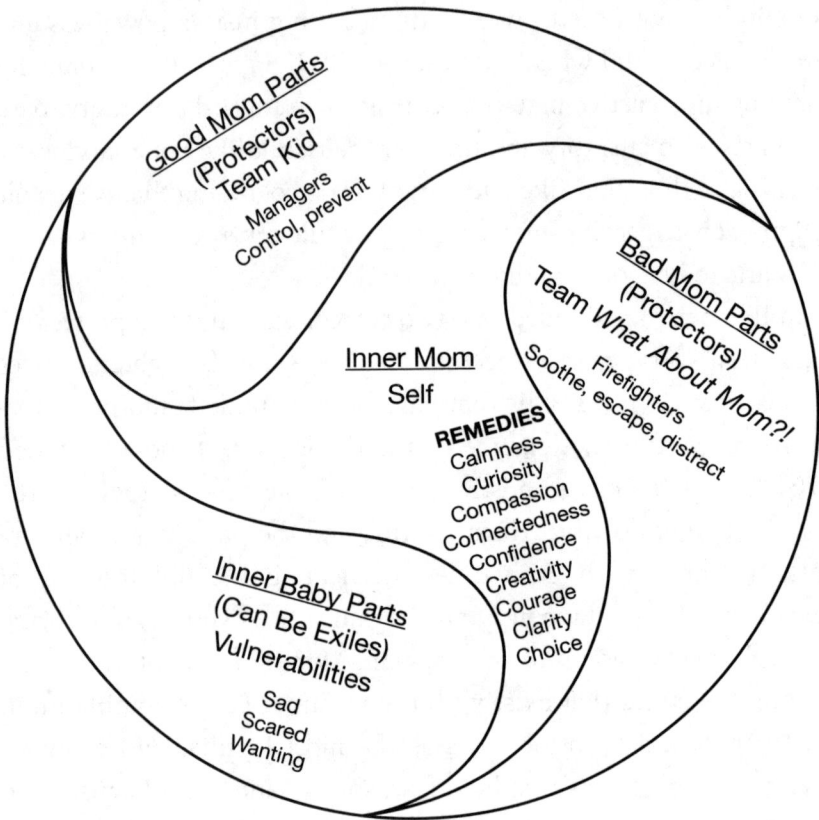

Good Mom Parts
(Protectors)
Team Kid
Managers
Control, prevent

Bad Mom Parts
(Protectors)
Team What About Mom?!
Firefighters
Soothe, escape, distract

Inner Mom
Self

REMEDIES
Calmness
Curiosity
Compassion
Connectedness
Confidence
Creativity
Courage
Clarity
Choice

Inner Baby Parts
(Can Be Exiles)
Vulnerabilities

Sad
Scared
Wanting

awareness inside of us and increase our flexibility so that we can tap into our own onboard wealth of compassion, calmness, and clarity.

Moms don't always vibe with the concept of "Self," but they totally get it when we talk about their "Inner Mom." As a mom, you have lots of experience being pushed way past your limit and yet still being able to find patience for your kids. You know in a deeply embodied way how it feels to be very present and wholeheartedly connected to someone small and vulnerable. There are times when your kids see you as their safe haven or as a steadying force. You know what it's like to be that kind of presence.

When we want moms to understand Self, we ask them to find their Inner Mom—the one who knows something about unconditional love. Want to try locating your Inner Mom?

JOURNAL

Think of a moment when you were really present for your child, just holding them or being a supportive presence when they needed your care—a time when you felt steady and patient, and you could feel your love for your child alive inside of you. Maybe you were surprised by your patience, or your capacity, not having encountered this kind of unconditional, connected caring within yourself before.

That's your Inner Mom. Step inside of her energy and look out through her eyes.

Now turn that beautiful Inner Mom energy around, so you're looking right at the parts of you who are tired, maxed out, embarrassed, angry, or afraid.

Let them see who you are now: a grown-up who has so much capability and such capacity for love and forgiveness. Let them feel your steady presence. You can introduce yourself…

Spend a moment journaling about the thoughts and feelings that emerge as you start to identify and embody your Inner Mom. What's it like to direct so much care toward yourself?

Some parts may feel hopeful; some may feel skeptical. Write down what you're noticing.

IFS lists qualities that are inherent to the Inner Mom and calls them the eight *C*'s of Self. We think of them as the gifts of your Inner Mom, and we call them "Remedies," adding in an additional fabulous *C* word—"choice"—with a nod to Senior IFS Trainer Cece Sykes, who loves the way Self widens our perspective and empowers us with options. Finding and accessing these internal resources is sort of the goal, if you will, of doing all this Mom Parts excavating. Just knowing you have your own Inner Mom onboard and that she has a whole host of beautiful Remedies to offer your parts is an empowering realization for us all.

All Mom Parts Welcome

In the words of Richard Schwartz, there are "no bad parts." So many of our parts have been conditioned to believe they are bad. Unwanted. Problematic. Shameful. Trouble. Too much. Not enough. We've internalized negative beliefs about our parts and gone on to live our entire lives operating from the mistaken belief that there's something wrong with us. There's not. It's such a huge relief to discover you're not bad and that you make sense.

This book is here to take the judgment and pathology out of "bad" Mom Parts, including parts that have aggressive feelings, like Anger, Fuck-it, Rage, and Resentful parts; or *negative* emotions, like Regret, Irritation, Depression, and Boredom. IFS gives us a way to experience our parts differently—as the well-intentioned, heroic inner beings that they are. Disassembling our conditioning around "good mom" behavior and giving ourselves permission to welcome the whole cast of inner characters is a game changer. Knowing your parts connects you to your authenticity and opens up a channel for your Inner Mom to help heal your wounds.

We're not singular minds that only feel and think one way. We have competing and conflicted parts of us that hold different agendas and specific fears and persistent hopes. All those mixed messages that churn inside of us will make us very uncomfortable—unless we know how to welcome the whole motley crew of voices and establish kind internal leadership in the form of our own Inner Mom. There is a way to find peace—or at least a genuine interest in all the different conflicting, apparently competing needs and impulses vying for attention inside of you.

While it's inarguably one of the most worthwhile, growth-inducing, important, and emotionally enriching paths a human being can move through, motherhood is also undeniably full of self-sacrifice and loss. Mothering is a grind. It's infuriating. Depleting. Boring. Thankless. That's just true. We as a culture have never looked kindly upon moms who talk seriously about the dark side of mothering that we all experience. Unhappiness in motherhood is disgraceful and stigmatized; we incorrectly view distressed mothers as being morally suspect. Moms who are sad or angry or who feel shaky and inadequate are seen as inferior. We act as though the mother-child relationship should be the one and only exception from every other relationship on earth, the singular relationship that exclusively generates positive feelings. Moms should never feel bad about mothering or dislike their children. But the truth is, motherhood and happiness don't go hand in hand. The way moral goodness and happy motherhood are conflated in the myths that are advertised to us creates a miserable, sometimes deadly trap for the 99.9 percent of us who do encounter real maternal unhappiness.

The reality is the mother-child relationship is a regular old relationship between two people who may or may not be temperamentally suited to each other. Or maybe they showed up in each other's lives at an inopportune time as is wont to happen on occasion. And then there are all the external circumstances that make mothering difficult, pertaining to lack of resources (sleep, time, money, energy, support). For so many reasons, motherhood can feel downright horrible at times, especially given the 24/7 demands of the job. Feeling bad isn't a crime. It's just how things are. Life is difficult, and relationships are complicated and imperfect. Even for moms. Especially for moms.

✴ It's normal to have all sorts of feelings about your child. It's acceptable to have a wide range of internal experiences related to motherhood. Welcome to reality.

If we don't have space to talk about and ventilate our difficult, distressed feelings about motherhood, we are forced to repress and suppress them, and that never actually works. Conversations about

Mom Parts need to be normal and welcome. Pushing down things that want to come up will only cause them to push back from below even harder. Your pain, if left untended, becomes unmanageable. It will take matters into its own desperate hands and demand center stage without bothering to get your consent. If you don't take care of your pain, it will do its best to take care of you, and it won't be graceful. It will look and feel *bad*.

The Moving Target of Good Mothering

Good moms feel awful when mothering suddenly requires something of us that we are unable to give. What our children need from us keeps changing over time, and certain developmental phases are better fits for some moms than others. When our kids' needs are basic, the job description is pretty clear. Being a good mom means feeding the hungry baby. Toddler scraped her knee and is crying? Hold her. Child has a nightmare? Check on them and soothe them back to sleep. In the early years, much of our work as moms centers around physical responsiveness to our little ones' reasonably straightforward needs. That doesn't mean it's easy work. Nor does it mean that what we're giving is simple or just transactional. It's not. Our responses are laden with information from our personal and ancestral histories. Our wordless, implicit communication with our very small children is perhaps the *most* meaningful, formative communication we will ever have with them. It matters so much. And yet all this bodily work and interaction we do with our tiny children feels reflexive, unconsidered, raw, unpolished, casual, even throwaway, as we move through the same routines again and again, bleary-eyed and half-asleep a good part of the time.

Yes, sometimes the crying seems to just go on and on without any real explanation, evading all of your efforts to make it better. In those early years, there's an endless list of needs to meet, and they all involve your emotional attunement and physical responsiveness. For some, the constant physical labor of the early years is the hardest phase of motherhood, as it tends to include less sleep, more bending over and chasing after, repetition, repetition, repetition, and not a lot of verbal engagement. It's exhausting, and did we mention it's repetitive? Early motherhood requires physical endurance and a sustained suspension of your own wants and needs. During these early years, moms can become disconnected from their former identities and lose touch with their sense of desire and aliveness. For some moms, it's these years that make us feel the worst.

EVELYN'S STORY

Evelyn feels good about herself as a mom. She feels connected to her three small children and has blown her own mind with the amount of patience and warmth she genuinely feels toward them most of the time. She wipes many snotty noses and poopy butts throughout the day, rescues kids who are about to topple down stairs or run into traffic, and sings the same songs and reads the same stories over and over, mostly breathing through it all and congratulating herself at the end of each long day for keeping all three small humans alive and relatively happy. But when the sun goes down and the house is quiet, she and her husband find themselves sitting on opposite ends of the couch, him with a beer and her with a pint of ice cream, not talking much and not connecting physically. "I just hope he doesn't try to touch me," she shares in therapy. "I just want to eat all the ice cream in the container and forget about the day and go into a cocoon of silence. And at the same time, I feel pretty sad and guilty not connecting with him."

Aside from being a good mom, Evelyn doesn't feel like she knows who she is anymore. She isn't interested in sex, she feels awkward in her body, she's not passionate about anything but keeping her kids healthy, and if she's honest, she's also really bored. Her minimal free time is spent recovering from the rigors of each day. "My husband still leaves the house every day and engages in adult conversations with people who admire him. I'm wearing the same pants for the third day in a row and planning how I might be able to clip my toenails later this week." She wonders if she will ever feel excited about her own existence again and gets teary when she thinks about how much she used to love dancing. "Honestly, I don't even know how I feel anymore, outside of protecting my kids. I love them but I don't love me."

Evelyn needed help reconnecting with parts of herself that existed beyond mothering. Speaking this nonjudgmental Mom Parts language gave her permission to be honest about feeling lost and disconnected from her pre-baby identity. Evelyn's inner judgment about being "selfish" for missing her old life began to soften, and she found the courage to ask her partner to take over bedtime routines twice a week so she could attend a dance class. "I realized my Caretaker parts had been so focused on the kids that I forgot I was still a whole person with a body that loves to move," she shared. As she began honoring both her mothering parts AND her other parts, Evelyn started to feel like herself again—not the person she was before kids, but a fuller, more integrated version who could be a devoted mother without completely disappearing.

Whereas the early years require a lot of physical responsiveness, mothering adolescents and adult children requires adjusting to your child's emerging boundaries. Where we used to move in for a much-needed hug, now we have to learn how to pull away and stand back out of respect for our budding adult's requests for privacy and separateness. Being the mom of teens and adults calls on a completely different skill set. The more-developed brains of older kids demand more-developed relational skills from parents. And for some moms, the teen years are the hardest and evoke the biggest sense of threat and failure. The threads of union we selflessly wove from the core of our being into the core of that child's being now belong to them. It takes a new kind of internal strength to watch your child pull the symbiotic threads apart one by one, casting off some of the sinew and marrow you donated to give them life. Being responsive and attuned to someone so autonomous and mysterious—who is learning to NOT need you and learning how to leave you—is a little bit hard for us. It can be excruciating for moms who were themselves abandoned.

The inborn *traits* of each of your children, including biological traits (appearance, activity level, special needs, sleep patterns, sensitivities, gender, etc.) as well as emotional and psychological traits (sociability, adaptability, reactivity, attention span, desire for closeness, etc.), bring out different parts of you as a mother. That's why you may feel like you're a better mom to one of your kids than to another, or a better mom to your kids at different stages of their development. Some moms are great with babies but really struggle with tweens and teens and vice versa. It's common to find the child who most resembles you to be the one you fret about or react to the most.

ASHA'S STORY

Asha is mom to eleven-year-old and eight-year-old daughters. "It's easier to be a good mom for my youngest daughter than my oldest. Is there something wrong with me? Olivia is so triggering for me. She's super defiant—I'll ask her to do something, and she just flat out says, 'I'm not gonna do it.' I get so furious! I can feel myself becoming like my mom, where I just want to annihilate her. I start yelling and I say really mean things. The part that wants to destroy her is so intense, but I eat my words because I know if I say those things, I WILL destroy her. Still, I can hardly look at her, I'm so mad...I feel like a terrible mom. I'm more like my mom than I ever wanted to be!

"My younger daughter is so much easier. She's less defiant, and I just don't get angry with her the same way I do with Olivia and I like her better. I feel like a monster for saying that, but it's true."

In therapy, Asha explores parts she identifies as her Blamer, Rage, and Inner Critic. As she spent time with these parts, she was able to name these Truths:

> *I don't always like being a mom.*
> *My kid really triggers my feelings of "I'm not good enough."*
> *Being a mom is really hard.*

Once Asha named these Truths, she became thoughtful. "Admitting these things makes me realize that underneath my Rage I'm feeling hurt and Scared—not just pissed off." Becoming aware of her hurt and fear seemed to slow something down inside her, and she got quiet. Asha was able then to speak to the shame she felt about "being such a mean mom." Because she felt new permission to explore her Bad Mom parts, she was able to go a step further. With tears in her eyes, she located a powerless part at the center of her reactivity. She called it "not mattering" and was able to remember feeling like she didn't matter to her parents as a child. She described her "not mattering" part like this:

> *I hate feeling this way.*
> *I don't exist.*
> *I don't even matter to anyone.*
> *I'm the worst person ever.*

Having this opportunity to uncover the deep pain beneath her "bad" behavior helped Asha understand herself. It made sense to her that being powerless was both terrifying and enraging as a child, and this helped her soften and get a little more curious about her reactions, rather than just coming down on herself. She noticed how Rage grabbed the wheel and got her Blamer yelling harsh words at Olivia. She saw how her Inner Critic made her "eat her words" to spare her daughter the worst of her Rage. And while eating her words was the last thing her Rage wanted to do, Asha expressed appreciation for her Inner Critic, who stopped her from doing worse damage—like the damage her parents did to her when they verbally abused her as a child. Asha shared that she felt more clarity now that she had this insight about how her parts were trying to help her.

✳ Our protector parts get triggered when they perceive a threat. But the threat isn't really our kids—it's a "tell" from our own Inner Baby. When we're triggered, we can pause and get curious about ourselves, rather than continue to see our kids as the source of our distress. IFS calls this "making a U-turn."

Many of our parts would like to change our kids and make them easier and less activating to the parts of us that feel scared, sad, and angry. But our kids need to feel unconditional love and support for who they are. When they feel rejected or unloved, they in turn develop their own parts, wisely working to shift their tender vulnerability out of harm's way. It turns out that the only way to authentically provide acceptance and presence to your child is to actively offer it to yourself first. By getting to know your Mom Parts, you start working with the stuff you *can* change and letting go of the futile effort to morph yourself and your kids into people who won't trigger you.

As your child develops, their vulnerabilities change. And the world we live in continues to evolve (hello, pandemic, climate change, social unrest, political upheaval...), bringing new challenges that intersect with your child's development in both complementary and confounding ways. Over the long stretch of motherhood, you will identify and experience new and different kid-based dangers and threats, which will stoke your anxiety and despair and then bring new relief and connection in the wake of upheaval.

As vulnerability and danger continue to shape-shift, your protectors will reorganize and reconfigure to address the job at hand. New parts push their way into leadership, making your old ways of coping and reacting obsolete and bringing in new protector parts in response to what you are now perceiving as vulnerability and as threat. Parts of ourselves we've never been acquainted with may show up, and once again, we are a strange new version of ourselves. Perhaps we don't recognize our child in the teen or adult who stands before us. And it's possible we also don't recognize ourselves in how we are feeling and reacting.

It's ridiculous that motherhood first demands boundaryless union from us, and then it does a one-eighty and asks us to surrender that union, just as selflessly. In the early years, it's *give me everything you've got*. In the later years, it's *get out of my space*. You have to be ALL in, 100 percent, and then removed, sometimes forcibly, often alternating with moments of interspersed union, but always on your child's timetable and in response to their developmental needs. Talk about triggering. If anything can evoke all kinds of hurt and protective parts in a human, it's got to be motherhood. Okay, maybe also childhood.

Parts show up in response to perceived threats. Parts protect vulnerability. Having a child multiplies your vulnerability times two (or more if you have multiple children). The more vulnerability that's present in your life, and the more threats you're perceiving, the more you need your protector parts—and the more extreme the protective response from your parts.

Impossible Standards

There's an ideal-mother archetype that we all seem to reference and compare ourselves to as we move through motherhood. That archetype is a merged conglomeration of the very best mothering we received as well as the kind of mothering we didn't receive and desperately wanted or needed. That ideal mom is someone who makes no mistakes. When we are made to feel entirely responsible for how our kids turn out, both physically (Feed them right!) and emotionally (Don't get upset! They're absorbing EVERYTHING you say and do!), we walk out of the pediatrician's office believing there's no room for mistakes and ashamed of all the ones we keep making. We walk out of the school office feeling judged, knowing they think we could be mothering better. We walk out of our grown child's dirty apartment feeling like our kid isn't living up to our expectations and blaming ourselves for not raising them well. Moms want to get it ALL right. Our kids are a reflection of us, and so our kids need to get it right too. We want acceptance and approval all around. Getting a B in motherhood is no longer good enough. We want to get an A and have clear affirmation that we're doing things exactly right. And in the pursuit of perfection, where the original good intention is to not fuck up your child, you miss out on being truly present, and you end up hurting yourself. You betray your own needs. You overwork and become more of a manager than a soulful human in a soulful relationship with a dependent, soulful person.

Baby- and child-centered consumerist cultures sell us on the idea that good moms have happy, healthy children who meet all their milestones, are socially solid, and don't get into self-harm or using drugs. They stay in touch after they move out, calling regularly, sending photos, and coming home on all the holidays. Your children should feel GREAT; they should love you and treat you with respect—if you're a good mom. It's made clear to us that it's mothers who are responsible for making good kids. It's on you. Your goodness rides on your child's wellness, intelligence, and happiness. The kid is a reflection of you. This child-centered definition of good mothering is an unfair setup for mothers who then work so hard at being good and at doing it right that the job itself destroys them. We wind up abandoning critical swaths of our own emotional truth, burning out and reaching regrettable breaking points. Enjoying our kid and enjoying ourselves become unattainable dreams because we get stuck in a loop of working too hard, suppressing our own needs, and feeling like we're always falling short. And it feels to us like everyone is watching and judging, especially other mothers.

With so many critical eyes on us, we don't just strive to be good moms; we aim for perfection. We are inundated with gorgeous, filtered images of moms at the top of their Pinterest game, doing Olympic-level mothering for kids who look a lot happier/better behaved/more successful and grateful than our kids, and the resounding impact is a budding realization that . . .

You're not good enough. You ~~could~~ should do better.

We have googleable access to alllll the information about pregnancy and child development and diagnoses. It's not hard to find what the norms and standards are for moms, babies, children, and families. Comparisons abound. *Am I doing this right? Is my kid normal?* We compare ourselves to other mothers, and we can tell there is, in fact, something wrong with us. Those moms look more confident, and their babies are eating/sleeping/pooping/rolling over in a way that ours isn't; their middle schoolers are getting good grades and eating carrots and kale; and their high schoolers are well-adjusted, high-performing athletes who are already being scouted by top colleges. Plus, the moms look happy. They aren't complaining, and they don't seem as anxious as we feel. What we feel is pissed off, inept, worried, and embarrassed. Failure is lurking nearby, and it wants in.

Motherhood calls upon us to lead dependent, vulnerable, highly reactive, less-developed human beings from helplessness toward capability. Toward safety. But also into expansion and growth. We need to give them everything we can but not so much that they never learn to do for themselves. We are tasked with accompanying our kids through thousands of mundane, repetitive moments as well as extraordinary life experiences, juggling conflicting goals of keeping them safe, supporting them in becoming contributing members of society, actualizing their talents, and helping them develop rich, meaningful relationships. We are responsible for all of this, and we feel the pressure of it. There are so many ways they need us to be attuned and responsive, including being attuned and responsive to all the ways they *don't* need us.

Oh my God.

And so, you don't always feel like a good-enough mom, regardless of how hard you try and regardless of how much your children love you. Chances are, despite what might appear to be a really solid showing, you feel guilty and ashamed of ways you've "failed" with your kids, probably as recently as this morning. And chances are, you get down on yourself about the kind of mom you are, either comparing yourself to other moms and coming up short or working extra hard to do things differently (i.e., better) pretty much every single day. Moms we see in our practices don't just strive for good enough—they aim for perfection and then blame themselves for every problem and disappointing outcome that inevitably crops up.

What We Hand Down

The good-mom archetype flavors our drinking water. We are all influenced by the pressures we feel from outside. And we are all carrying the weight of our mothers' Good Mom and Bad Mom parts inside of us too, in the form of memories, values, fears, and longings. If our moms were wonderful, we feel inspired, pressured perhaps, to be that same kind of wonderful mother ourselves. We have an example of what good mothering looks and feels like, and we aim to match it. Can we ever possibly measure up? Are we coming through for our kids the way our own moms came through for us?

And if our moms were less than wonderful, we feel inspired, pressured perhaps, to *not* be like her, to distinguish ourselves as totally different—as really good moms. We have a lived example of what bad mothering looks and feels like, and we aim to avoid it. And how do we know when we, as apples, have fallen far enough from that bad-mom tree? Is our goodness determined by whether our kids adore us? Is it determined by how successful our kids are? By how self-sacrificing we are? Or by the egregiousness of the mistakes we've made? Mothers who have survived childhood neglect and abuse are haunted and pursued by potent mandates to never repeat the horrors of their own past. Every average mom mistake gets filtered through an unforgiving lens.

We carry information about mothering in our parts, and we pass that information to our children through how we touch them, how we feel toward them, the things we say, and the look in our eyes when we're serious or sad or worried. We tell them all about mothering without using any words, through the way we stuff their little limbs into their pj's, how we greet them in the morning, and how we respond to their mistakes, bad grades, and their rejection of us. Every day we're teaching them—*Here's how good mothering looks and feels (or doesn't look and feel)*—the same way we were taught. We hand down what we know, what we wish, and what's missing through the way we mother.

✳ It's highly motivating to be self-compassionate when we realize that softening toward ourselves translates directly to helping our kids.

Mothercentered AF

And what about you? What about mom? Yes, the disheveled one in the background who seldom gets noticed or inquired into. The one who's often running late but manages to do more by 11 a.m. than she used to do in an entire day. The one who worries about her own deteriorating mental health but doesn't ever quite get to making the phone call to the therapist who specializes in supporting moms, because she's so busy trying to hit all the marks while momming. The one who thought she would get to take a long walk today out in the sunshine but ended up home with a sick kid, folding laundry instead. Yeah, that one.

Yes, your body accepted this small life into itself, or in the case of adoption, fostering, and stepmomming, agreed to host the small life, but likely without the consent of all your parts. You probably have some parts that weren't thrilled about giving up solo space to take on a lifetime of mothering. Just because you're hosting this separate life doesn't mean you've ceased to be your own individual self. You are still a separate person. Even while you are merged. Even when you can't tell that you're separate—you are. And because you're a person, you have parts that are interested in your own wellness and your own perspective. Your own vision and preferences. All of your self-interest is still here, even though it may get very little airtime or attention.

So now you have parts that are dedicated to caring for your baby or child with incredible focus and commitment, even after they become adults or move away. And you also have parts that remember who you are, separate from being a mom—and those parts care about you more than they care about your kid. Having parts with very differing agendas (kid versus you) is the source of much strife for moms. Learning to engage compassionately with your parts who have opposed agendas is a way to bring more internal peace into your life. We're here to welcome you back to yourself. We call this welcoming of all your Mom Parts being mothercentered. We're all about centering moms. We're mothercentered AF.

Mothercentering is an approach that beholds and respects a mother's subjective experience with interest, recognizing and valuing how *she* sees and feels things as central to her and her family's health. Without excluding the interests and needs of her children, mothercentrism expects and welcomes the polarized parts inside of moms that are tasked with holding and juggling the competing needs of mothers and their children. This is normal, workable mom stuff: parts that prioritize your children and parts that protect your own self-interest. Parts make sense. We know how to work with them. Let's do this.

Chapter 2

Motherhood Is a Portal

Pregnancy, birth, and the postpartum period aren't gentle. Shepherding a new life into the world brings us face-to-face with dependency, pain, fear, and mortality. We are witness to the vulnerability of our tiny baby, whose fragility and sensitivity take over our awareness completely as we feel the responsibility of keeping this little person alive.

We all know that babies are vulnerable, but what we don't seem to collectively comprehend is just how vulnerable new moms are too. New moms and their babies rely on care from outside to stay safe and to be well. And human needs are nonnegotiable. When a baby's needs are not sufficiently met, the baby may not survive and cannot thrive. Similarly, when a new mom's needs are not sufficiently met, she may not survive and cannot thrive. This period of increased vulnerability requires responsive, attuned care—for both members of the dyad. Good care is the kind of care that bestows power and respect on an otherwise powerless person. Babies and moms both need that kind of care.

Your experience of getting pregnant, being pregnant, giving birth, and the quality of your postpartum life affect the kind of mom you become.

JOURNAL

What was it like giving birth? How was your early experience of becoming a mom? Did you feel respected? Were you held

by people you trusted? Were you alone? Did you feel seen and understood? How did you get through it? What's the story you tell about those early days?

Like babies, pregnant and postpartum women are physically and emotionally vulnerable in startling ways. On a very basic level, they're larger and slower, their joints are looser, and they're usually tired. They can't run from enemies or defend themselves as effectively as they could before their physiology changed and they grew this belly or birthed this infant or started breastfeeding through sleepless nights. They're bound to their baby. They rely on other people to find food and bring it to them, to ward off danger and help keep them out of the jaws of predators. And babies are even more defenseless; they're small and helpless, also unable to escape from danger or find food on their own. They can't coordinate movement in their bodies to scratch an itch or shift positions. They can't speak. Babies are helpless and vulnerable.

Vulnerability has to do with openness. Brené Brown defines **vulnerability** as "uncertainty, risk, and emotional exposure."[1] When we're vulnerable, the tender parts of us are exposed, revealed, and permeable. In our openness and vulnerability, there is the glorious possibility of being seen and known deeply and accurately, and of feeling accepted and loved for who we really are. In our openness and vulnerability, there is also the possibility of being hurt and wounded, since our tenderness is so visible and accessible. As sentient beings, we are all vulnerable, whether we like it or not, to varying degrees throughout our lives. When it isn't safe to be vulnerable, our protector parts will do their very best to build barriers around our tenderness, trying to dial back our sensitivity or amp up our control. When vulnerability has been established to be a reasonably safe state or a worthwhile endeavor, our protector parts don't have to muscle up quite so much or become as extreme. Our systems learn that it's fine to be open and that tenderness feels good. We have more ease and familiarity with our authentic selves and with connection and intimacy.

Vulnerability is required for connection. It's required for secure attachment. To feel seen, known, and attached to another person, the tender parts of us need to be involved. We have to exist with a certain amount of openness to reach out and to be reached into. When our vulnerability is held with respect and kindness, we become our best selves. Vulnerability is then a superpower that imbues our actions and relationships with heart and realness, making for a richer and more connected life.

✳ Vulnerability + Respect = Good Health

If you grew up in a war zone with abusive caregivers, vulnerability won't be as accessible to you. You learned that when your tenderness is exposed, you get hurt. When you were helpless, you were harmed. It was dangerous to be open and honest about your true needs and feelings, so you figured out the best way to limit your exposure. Your manager parts emerged to help you find alternatives to helplessness. Even though as an adult you are no longer helpless, even now, when vulnerability visits you, you're reminded of how helpless and threatened you were as a child. Your system gets anxious and starts bracing for attack. You've learned to avoid being vulnerable.

Helplessness is dangerous. As an infant and a child, you ARE helpless—you cannot fend for yourself. When you are unable to help yourself and you feel threatened, parts of you will show up spontaneously to protect you. These protector parts are ready for action, here to fashion any and every possible barricade between you and the threat. In the face of threat, we move into the stress responses of fight, flight, freeze, or fawn, which are descriptive of the kinds of protectors that are dominant inside of us. Certain protectors will be more effective in specific moments, and those will climb into the driver's seat with the intention of keeping our tenderness as far away from danger as possible. They help us escape, fight back, shut down, appease, or dissociate from the frightening world around us.

Critical developmental needs go unmet when you aren't cared for or respected as a child. Those unmet needs travel with you through time, and they take on an icky tone of worthlessness, badness, or unlovability. You come up with a story and a way of understanding your unmet needs that always includes some rendition of *I don't matter, I'm unlovable, I have no value, I'm bad.* This is what children naturally and organically do to preserve relationships with their caretakers. Kids believe their unmet needs are a reflection of their own badness and failure. Children must preserve faith in their caretakers because they know they cannot take care of themselves. So in childhood, the healthiest, most adaptive choice we have is to identify ME as the problem and as the source of the badness. Believing we're bad and unlovable is also a gigantic, fundamental error that becomes the root of much ongoing emotional distress. The assumption of our own innate badness is called shame.

✴ Vulnerability + Harm = Fear and Shame

When your needs aren't perfectly met, but your pain is acknowledged as valid and real, good things happen. Your vulnerability can be safely experienced. It doesn't morph into a deeper sense of powerlessness and shame that must then be guarded. Moms, listen up!

> ✴ In mothering, there's plenty of room to make mistakes with our kids. We can screw up—and we can repair. Humans are resilient—we just require that our truth be seen and respected.

But when your needs are not met and you never get to learn about or speak aloud the truth, validity, soulfulness, and righteousness of your parts, then your vulnerability closes up shop, locks the door, and flips the OPEN sign to CLOSED. You become identified with your protectors. You become Controlling, Anxious, Depressed, Panicky, or Suicidal—because those parts of you decided they need to be here on behalf of the vulnerability they guard. Your system has determined that it's better to be fortified with defenses than to be powerless and vulnerable. Makes sense, right?

When Boundaries Dissolve

Boundaries define people and parts. A boundary is a line separating where one thing ends and a unique and separate thing begins, with its own specific and particular nature. Having boundaries is critical to survival and to health and existence. We move through life with all sorts of boundaries in place: emotional boundaries, physical boundaries, conversational boundaries, boundaries around time and around energy use. Every single one of these boundaries is compromised by motherhood.

Not having boundaries, or having permeable, flexible boundaries, is critical to reproduction: Sperm must find a way to permeate an egg's membrane. Blastocysts must penetrate the wall of the uterine lining and force their way in, embedding themselves in their host—welcomed or not. The fetus must find a way to break out of the confines of Mom's uterus, breaching her cervix, which has to dilate ten freaking centimeters(!) to allow passage of this creature—or via surgical incision, slicing skin and muscle and uterus(!), bulldozing her bodily boundaries. Once a woman is pregnant, she no longer has a distinct, separate self that is exclusively under her own jurisdiction. Having clear distinction between where one thing ends and another thing begins is what keeps us differentiated and defined—oriented to who we are and what we're doing with our bodies in time and space. Our immune systems are a kind of boundary, keeping out unwanted viruses and germs so that we stay well. But during pregnancy, our immune system is co-opted by a new director—the fetus—who commandeers a series of physiological changes that keep the baby (a foreign body containing foreign DNA) from being rejected. Our own biological protective mechanisms are loaned out and not entirely available to us. Our boundaries give way to allow for a collaborative and cooperative endeavor that doesn't seek our informed consent.

So, what happens when Mom's boundaries dissolve or give way? How does she hang on to her own distinct being as she's loaning out very personal and highly valuable regions of herself in ways that compromise her? How does she adjust adaptively in a manner that honors and supports her existence, while allowing the boundaries of that existence to morph and shape-shift?

Beyond pregnancy, boundaries continue to be porous. Moms' bodies are used as a food source, comfort animal, jungle gym, emotion regulator, first responder, cleaner, groomer, and then later as a nutritionist, chauffeur, therapist, and financial adviser. Our nervous systems, meaning our ability to feel, sense, metabolize, soothe, interpret, react, catch, release, and respond, are shared, maybe equally, between our children and ourselves. We belong to them in ways we can't negotiate. They have access to us in ways no one else ever has or ever will.

It's not easy. Nor is it "natural." It's uncomfortable and triggering. Because our boundaries are diffuse, we are more vulnerable. Where we used to feel guarded, supported, impenetrable, indifferent, or immune, we no longer do. The most tender parts of us are revealed, and they exist now, at least in part, outside of our bodies and outside of our control. We are exquisitely vulnerable now, to love and healing and also to harm and loss. We lack certain filters; we feel more.

As women, we have been conditioned to view our desire for boundaries with distrust. Having boundaries, saying NO, and setting limits have long been associated with being "difficult," "uppity," or a "bitch." This plays out in a new mom's feelings about how to draw lines with family members and in-laws and people who want to touch the belly or hold the baby or offer unsolicited advice when she's not asking for it. How does she find and hold boundaries, now that her system has dissolved so many of them and the world wants to intrude? And how does this unboundaried experience of hosting new life *not* lead to some form of mental health struggle or crisis?

JOURNAL

For moms who are beyond the early years, what is the status of your personal boundaries these days? Can you feel your separate self once again? Are you able to say no as needed? What feelings come up in you when your boundary lines get crossed? In what ways do you still feel merged with your child?

A Wild Reconfiguration of Parts

When a mom's physiology changes and familiar boundaries dissolve, vitally important *parts* of her inner world are forced to reconfigure. Protective and connective energies take up residence in new ways. Old protector parts are displaced, causing Mom to feel raw and exposed. New protector parts jump into the driver's seat and start steering, almost always in an anxious, baby-centered direction. Critical, judgmental parts latch on to the anxious parts, tracking errors and pushing for improvement to ensure Mom does her very important job the *right* way. The re-org in parts leadership dramatically changes Mom's focus, priorities, and felt sense of being in the world. She is no longer who she used to be. She feels vulnerable and dependent in her morphing body, and she assumes new responsibility for her child in a full-throttle kind of way. The reconfiguration of Mom Parts trends toward hyperarousal, which can be hard on Mom's mental and physical health. Self-energy can become difficult to access.

It's common for people to talk about the struggle of new motherhood as an "imbalance," and the assumption is that the imbalance just has to do with hormones or biology. But a more holistic, mothercentered perspective provides another way of looking at (new) mothers' suffering—as an imbalance or destabilization in internal leadership, contributed to by culture, social context, physiology, and the demands of her new job. Her parts have been thoroughly rearranged and repurposed, and the net result is that she feels like a stranger to herself.

We have observed that moms deal with feelings of powerlessness and vulnerability in one of two ways: with protector parts or with Inner Mom (Self) energy. These are the two internal resources we have available to us. Two choices—it's that simple.

MOM'S TWO INTERNAL RESOURCES:

♡ Protector parts

♡ Inner Mom

Having this clarity gives us some direction for working with our big reactions. It's helpful to understand that beneath all protectors there is a big helping of vulnerability and, possibly accompanying it, a generous side of powerlessness. When we can appreciate that our reactions and responses in the present day are being informed by our early experiences of powerlessness, compassion flows much more readily. We aren't assholes. We aren't liars. We aren't bad. We got scared, and our protector parts showed up, ready to defend the small, powerless child we once were alongside the child we are now mothering. We can start to trust that underneath our "bad" behavior there is fear and vulnerability. And we can start cultivating curiosity and interest in welcoming our protectors and hearing their stories, knowing that they are fundamentally innocent. (Yes, even our Rage part.)

When we're young and our vulnerability is not met and held with respect—when we are physically harmed, abandoned, rejected, or humiliated—we split off that piece of ourselves, disowning but also, in a sense, protectively hiding that locus of tenderness. Our protectors then work very hard to keep that injured spot exiled out of awareness and to keep us on track in the hopes that we will never have to endure that kind of injury again. Being scared and getting hurt will always call forth our protector parts, who assume the job of keeping us alive and keeping us connected to the people who matter most to us.

We all come into motherhood chewing on our personal histories, full of beliefs, hopes, fears, and expectations related to the lives we've already lived. We've got the taste of our own childhood in our mouths, and it may or may not be a pleasant one. Even when we're at our most empowered and resilient, our past flavors our experience of our present. But when we are profoundly affected and dismantled, as we are by matrescence, our past comes rushing back in, unbidden.

The residual tone of your early experiences of family and connection shows up again in your relationship with your child and in the family you create as an adult. How you felt as a child will emerge in the present, which can feel surprising and sometimes upsetting for moms who were expecting something different. Motherhood may not come with a printed owner's manual, but for better or worse, it always calls forth a how-to guide from our own embodied wisdom. We know how to parent based on how we were parented—what we witnessed and experienced as children from the people who raised us.

Your kids can cause you to feel disempowered and helpless lightning fast—by crying incessantly, throwing tantrums in the grocery store, being impolite with teachers, staying out too late, getting tattoos, and not calling when they said they would.

JOURNAL

When your child defies or ignores or disappoints you, how do you deal with the feeling of powerlessness and the lump that sinks in your belly? Do you get mad and lash out? Do you collapse and break down? Do you disappear and check out? How do you greet your powerlessness and your vulnerability?

Physiology and the Perinatal Portal

Reproduction has a mandate, and though elegant in ways, it's not gentle on a mother's body or psyche. The physiology of matrescence opens a portal to your past, ushering in all kinds of important information that moms need in order to relate to and bond with their babies. As that emotion-rich material surfaces (and it REALLY SURFACES postpartum), moms are forced to contend with it. Those big emotions almost always include the following:

- intense fears
- more tenderness and tears
- gigantic hopes and expectations
- bigger protective reactions
- lots of grief

Moms experience a true "nervous system expansion"[2] when their physical, emotional, and spiritual bodies stretch to accommodate and account for an additional (highly dependent) life. That nervous system expansion includes a massive reconfiguration of parts of you—which is über-growth-inducing but also incredibly unsettling. Matrescence pulls forth some of the most primitive, difficult, and confusing psychological experiences of a person's life. Moms do, in a sense, become babies alongside their babies.

Anyone who has mothered an infant will tell you that every bit of their unfinished emotional business reappeared, front and center, upon the birth of their child. How and why does this happen?

Symbiosis—oneness—between a mom and her baby is a prerequisite for a baby's health and development. Symbiosis is a costly donation for moms. With the dissolution of Mom's boundaries comes the opening of a literal and metaphorical portal designed to help Mom download all her stored knowledge about connection and dependency and vulnerability. The *perinatal portal* establishes a spiritual, psychological, and energetic connection from Mom's present to her implicit, embodied past. Implicit knowledge—meaning the stuff she can't necessarily find words for but deeply and intimately knows—has been stored subcortically, out of conscious awareness. Her own early attachment experiences are unearthed, and her blueprint for intimate relationships and emotion regulation appears, ready to be handed down. That blueprint holds the fine details of Mom's sense of belonging, which now shifts front and center in her psyche, brought in by the undertow of maternal physiology. Where there is unprocessed trauma in Mom's early, unconscious memories, it will reemerge in motherhood, lapping at the shore of her awareness, depositing images, sensations, and emotions in its wake. If Mom was well nurtured and cared for as a child, she is swept up in a gentler undertow, one that holds her safely buoyant in its salty warmth.

When the perinatal portal opens, the maternal brain becomes malleable and receptive to new learning; it is catapulted by motherhood into old material, but with new possibilities for healing. Mom's brain changes dramatically and prunes itself to better meet the demands of the moment. Studies using neuroimaging technology show that becoming a mother triggers brain changes as extensive as those seen in teenagers, with long-lasting modifications to regions managing emotional bonds, threat detection, and caregiving responses.[3] The science confirms what mothers have always known: Becoming a parent fundamentally rewires who you are at the most basic biological level. Those changes show up subjectively in moms feeling more emotional, less verbal, more tuned in to their bodies and their intuition and less attached to time and to logic. It makes sense that the more effectively moms can channel and interpret infant cues and vibes, the easier it will be to respond to an infant's needs in an attuned way.

In the space that exists between mother and child, there is a commingling of past and present. Moms who've suffered childhood attachment trauma will absolutely revisit that trauma, viscerally and somatically, through mothering their children. The events of the present moment are filtered through Mom's catalog of memories, snagging on painful points and sailing deftly through smoother waters. Moms have no control over the memories bursting forth—but we do have agency over how we engage with them. For those of us who had painful childhoods, the bad news is we bring our past into the present with our children. And the good news is we can bring our present into the past now, to heal our Inner Baby.

TINA'S STORY

Tina is two months postpartum with her first child. She's struggling with insomnia, and her mood is tanking as she begins to string together multiple weeks of very fragmented sleep. Tina shares that her baby cries a lot, and she feels like a failure when she can't soothe the crying away. Through tears, she recounts her birth story, which didn't go the way she had expected. "I wanted an unmedicated birth, but the baby was in distress and I had to have a C-section. Then she spent the first two days in the NICU without me. I feel like I failed my baby right out of the starting gates." Tina says that she's feeling depressed, and she thinks her baby would be better off with a different mother who "knows what she's doing."

"The one thing I'm doing well is nursing. This baby is an excellent eater and she won't take a bottle, so I'm here pretty much round the clock, feeding her and comforting her between cry fests. I can't fall asleep at night—my mind is racing and my body won't settle. I feel like crap, I dread the nights, and if I'm honest, I'm feeling some suicidal feelings too. I just don't want to keep repeating nights like these. They're brutal. My partner wants me to wean the baby so she can take over feeding her, but I just can't. It's the one thing I'm doing well. It feels like a horrible and cruel decision to have to make—either take away this one area where I'm able to be a good-enough mom or never sleep again. Right now, I'm not willing to stop nursing her. And yes, I'm kind of losing my mind."

Tina needed help addressing her lack of sleep, which meant changing things in her physical and external world and bringing in her partner to develop a concrete plan for helping Tina sleep at night. Once she was sleeping more, she had more capacity to dig into her parts and explore what she uncovered as wounds from her own early childhood.

"I feel like my daughter is going to hate me. My mom was always pretty irritable, and I never felt really safe with her when I was small. I'm afraid that's what my daughter feels toward me. I can't comfort her sometimes. She just cries and cries, and I sit there crying too, feeling like I have nothing to give her and she knows it. I'm not a real mom. I don't know how to do this." Many tears were shed as Tina began to explore her fears about being like her mom and her grief around not enjoying new motherhood. She could feel her own Inner Baby parts who needed more care. Speaking this nonjudgmental Mom Parts language gave her permission to be honest about feeling vulnerable and "needy." Tina's self-judgment cooled, and she found the courage to ask her extended family for more support and TLC, which brought her relief and helped her ease into a more relaxed state where she could start to differentiate between her own Inner Baby's story and the spectacular mothering she was providing her baby girl.

Intergenerational Healing

Whatever imprints a mom carries will reemerge in her relationship with her child(ren), offering an opportunity to share historical, generational legacies, for better or for worse. When you bring your past into the present with your child, you get to draw on all the love and care that you were fortunate to receive. You get the privilege of handing down the sustaining legacy of your family line so that your child will continue to receive that beautiful intergenerational wealth. But if your past was less wholesome, bringing it into the present with your child means bringing in your unresolved pain. In the space between you and the clean slate that is your child, you are adding historical colors and ancestral textures and wordlessly asking your child to contend with it all.

So many moms we encounter are zealously committed to NOT handing down their painful family legacies. They attempt to avoid territories of heartache and tragedy by doing a complete one-eighty and parenting in ways that are opposite of the parenting they received. It turns out this kind of deliberate avoidance is still a form of transmitting trauma. By only staying on "good" streets and avoiding the "bad" streets in the neighborhood of our inner psyches, we inadvertently pass down the same fear, reactivity, and fear-based rejection of vulnerability that we learned and endured as children. Though packaged differently, the handing down of unprocessed pain is always the handing down of unprocessed pain. When moms haven't had the opportunity to discover and behold what they endured as children and haven't had the benefit of healing from those wounds, they share those familiar wounds.

Moms are biologically and evolutionarily tasked with imprinting their baby's nervous system, using their own as a reference point. Babies learn what to expect through repeated interactions with their mother (or primary caregiver). What Mom experienced in the way of trauma, neglect, and abuse—or warmth, safety, and connection—will flood her system and set the tone for the long motherhood journey that lies ahead. Moms consult their own Inner Baby as they engage with their real baby. And the wisdom of their own lived experience pulls from the imprint of their mother, and her mother before her, extending back through many generations.

Intergenerational healing can only come when moms are in an atmosphere of safety and care. When moms can draw on abundant resources in their present-day lives, they can give their children the best versions of themselves. They can send care packages consisting of the wellness they feel in their present lives back in time to their own Inner Babies, who may still be wounded. This is the magical healing power of motherhood. If moms are resourced enough to feel what they couldn't afford to feel as children, they're poised for healing.

So here's the bad news: Moms get immersed in emotional material that's laden with all sorts of intense vulnerability, still rocking with aftershocks from past traumas. Motherhood puts our unfinished business under a microscope and commands our full attention.

And here's the good news: Motherhood gives us an opportunity to revisit and redo our early imprints. Through the intimate experience of mothering our children, we are reacquainted with innocence, dependency, openness, and helplessness. We remember what it is to need someone else so absolutely and to have no power to defend and protect ourselves. Holding our children's preciousness is powerful motivation to heal, so we don't have to repeat a painful past and so we can provide a nourishing experience for our families, which in turn heals our parts.

✳ **Motherhood gives us an opportunity to revisit and redo our early imprints.**

Through the perinatal portal, the past is connected to the present, and moms can rewrite their attachment stories. Legacy burdens can be transformed into legacy gifts and heirlooms that will bless our families for generations to come. It's a unique phase of life and a time of massive brain rewiring, when deep, lasting healing can happen.

When Your Protectors Take the Wheel

Moms who don't feel well supported (inside or outside) will get caught in an experience of survival threat—they shift out of connection and into protection mode. Their protectors take over, and Mom is no longer available for attunement, which means her little one has no mature, auxiliary nervous system to help regulate and stabilize them. Children's brains require attunement from an external, developed, synchronized, caring brain. Without that kind of attunement, babies and children have their own experience of survival threat.

For optimal social health, humanity needs to support mothers so that they can be vulnerable and maximally interconnected with their children. But moms often find themselves undercared for and underresourced, living in protection mode. It turns out our nervous systems operate in a fairly binary manner when it comes to survival threat—either we ARE experiencing threat and defending ourselves or we AREN'T. Sometimes moms are experiencing present-day threats to safety, sufficient care, or adequate resources. It's pretty hard to unblend from parts that are up around real and present threats—and it's also not particularly wise. We need our protectors when danger is near.

Moms also dip into emotions and memories that *feel* threatening but are not reflective of real and present dangers. They experience historical, implicit survival threats, as attachment and relational memories emerge from the perinatal portal. Remembering and feeling historical threats from past abuse, neglect, or trauma can push a sleep-deprived, stressed-out mom into protection mode.

From Powerless to Powerful

The following chapters are dedicated to helping you get to know your parts so that you can start to give them the best possible care from inside yourself. The world outside might continue to suck, but you can be a love machine inside. You can lavish yourself with compassion and tenderness every single day. Sometimes the term "self-care" can feel hollow or shallow. But working with your Mom Parts is deep systemic care—like taking your psychological system to the manufacturer and getting an update and a reset. You discover what your own parts genuinely need from you to feel understood and respected. You consult yourself—and determine what's true for you. You listen to your own inner guidance and follow the path that your parts lead you on. With a little direction from us, you learn how to hold your most painful feelings and share the good news with them—that you're bigger now, that you have greater capacity and more choices. You have a voice, and you can move your body. You might even have credit cards, transportation, and a stash of dark chocolate, as well as people who love you whom you can call on for support.

✵ **The reservoir of love that has manifested for your child is here for your own use too.**

Being able to connect to the resources you have in the present day, and to the power that comes with being an adult, allows you to update your parts. You can send the good news inward, to your vulnerable and powerless parts who experienced such painful injuries:

You are not alone anymore. There is a mother here, with so much warmth and love to offer you. She can help you now.

Chapter 3

Mothering from the Inside Out

We bring our unfinished emotional business with us into mother-hood. Every single one of us gets slammed with the intensity of our own vulnerability in those early months. And then, every step of the way, we reencounter our young selves, through synchronizing and empathizing with our children. When our kids are babies, we co-experience helplessness and dependency with them. When they're toddlers, we start to feel the emotional tone of our own toddlerhood as we witness our little ones enter the phase of life where they begin moving willfully in the direction of their own choosing. And then as childhood progresses through adolescence, we relive the painful events and the joyful yearnings of those formative years, watching from the sidelines as our kids struggle and fail and accomplish, awash in a flood of our own remembering. We don't know in advance that we will be playing back the recording of our childhood and reliving all the highlights and low points in full color as we mother our kids. For some of us, this is joy, realized and actualized. We get to recycle all the love we received and then share it with the small people we're introducing into the world. For all of us, reexperiencing the shitty moments from our past is hard.

When your perinatal portal opened, it was as if a psychological dam lifted, and ancient, primitive feelings were suddenly permitted to come rushing into your psyche. As a new mom, you were taken over by primal, emotionally charged parts that showed up in your physical body, colored your mood, and supercharged your thoughts with baby-centered concerns and preoccupations. Your former sense of self used to be constructed by a familiar set of protectors who reliably helped you function and feel "normal." Those old protectors who were dialed in to guarding your pre-baby sense of self got whisked away in the night. They got caught in the tidal wave sweeping in from the perinatal portal and were replaced by a different set of protectors who are called to action by new baby-related vulnerabilities. These foreign protector parts show up ready to take care of business. They're aware that a new baby is on the scene—but the wild thing is they can't distinguish between the new baby you're mothering outside of you and the baby you once were, who still exists inside of you. They just know things have gotten very...well...vulnerable around these parts. They tune their ears to the changed environment, assessing for threat and safety in highly sensitized ways, determined to miss nothing and catch everything.

These protectors arrive in response to activity in the "emotional right hemisphere" of your maternal brain, which is more connected with the emotional state of your baby, according to Allan Schore, a clinician-scientist who has been a massive contributor to the field of understanding the neuroscience of attachment processes between babies and their mothers.[1] It's this right-hemisphere shift that connects you to a felt sense of your baby's wordless experience. And perhaps it's this right-hemisphere shift that causes you to blend with your own Inner Baby parts—the ones that hold emotion and history pertaining to your experience as a fetus, a newborn, and an infant. The shift away from the verbal, logical, and linear world of left-brain dominance is necessary for us as new moms to wire our nervous systems to our infants' so we can meet their needs and teach them how to be human beings.

Leading with our left brain creates a more familiar and typical inner adult state that moms miss keenly in their postpartum months. Remember how *off* you felt in those early months? You were used to existing in a world where words, time, and reason were your currency. All that logical, linguistic luxury went into the garbage can when you had a newborn. Your old BFF protectors were left-brain guys who knew how to help you find comfort and avoid your triggers in that pre-baby landscape. But these new protectors are from the other side of the tracks, and they're primitive, emotional, relentless, and most of all, vulnerable.

The State of Your Inner Baby

Mom's "Inner Baby" is a made-up psychological construct we use to describe the wild vulnerability that moms bring to motherhood from their own personal history of dependency and powerlessness. Having a felt sense of your own Inner Baby gives you the ability to resonate with your infant in a wordless, embodied way, which keeps you in developmental lockstep with your fetus/baby/child through time. As you relate to your own implicit memories from early life, you encounter intense primal material that activates around safety and lack of safety, worth and worthlessness, enough and not enough, hunger and satiation, ease and agitation, contentedness and despair. You are privy to pretty much all the most intense emotions and sensations a human can have. As a result, symptoms, or unsettled parts, are very likely to resurface in your system. If you were safe and well loved as a baby, and your physical and emotional needs were met with care, your Inner Baby will be a repository of a fair amount of yumminess. You will have a deep well to draw from as you hand down your family legacy of safety and connectedness. Yes, there are still all the major struggles of motherhood, but you will likely feel more resourced as you meet them. Even still...your Inner Baby is intensely vulnerable because guess what: You're a human being! Every single one of us has holes in the fabric of our security. Regardless of how beautifully we were mothered and parented, and no matter how trauma-free our past was, everyone has insecurities and areas of extraordinary tenderness.

And motherhood reveals every tiny hole in your security blanket and brings it into stark relief—even for very well-adjusted moms.

Some moms feel like their upbringing was pretty fantastic—so why are they struggling? Becoming a mom is like getting a close-up under the hood and really getting to see, often for the first time, how all the pieces fit/don't fit together. Just as life is requiring us to work with the quirky child we got, it's also requiring us to work with the quirky system we have, which includes our own neurological uniqueness. And while most parents are loving and well meaning, it's inevitable that we will all emerge into adulthood with at least a few missing pieces.

But what if on top of your quirky system, you didn't get the care you needed as a baby or child? When we're born to parents who are struggling with their own unmet needs, there just aren't enough emotional groceries to feed the family. If Mom or Dad is in bad shape, kids aren't well taken care of. If we were required to meet our parents' needs as children, our own needs had to get pushed to the back burner, maybe even taken completely off the stove. We focused instead on trying to keep our parents in one piece, in the hope that we ourselves might receive some scraps of love and care. As a result, our Inner Babies are lying in wait, still hungry to receive what they need, and we, like the generations before us, come to expect that our children will meet those needs for us, the same way we were required to meet our parents' emotional needs. Our hungry beaks are open and lunging at our kids, looking for affirmation of our goodness and lovability. Only, kids are not equipped to provide emotional sustenance to their parents without being injured. Kids provide care to their parents when they understand that they must. Kids who get parentified (turned into miniature, underdeveloped caretakers) grow protectors that manage, suppress, and inhibit their own needs. Because they must. And suppressing and inhibiting their own needs comes at a huge cost to children. They carry those unmet needs forward in time, stored in their psyches in the form of their own Inner Baby.

MOM'S INNER BABY

- Represents your vulnerability and dependency
- Holds implicit memory of your formative experience of safety, love, and connection
- Embodies your unmet needs
- Supports symbiosis and attunement with your child
  - Resonates with empathy
  - Keeps you in developmental lockstep
- Is the nexus at which your past meets your child's present

Understanding Inner Baby Parts

Inner Baby parts are FEELING parts. We've simplified the Inner Baby down to three primary parts: Sad, Scared, and Wanting. These three parts hold the tenderness of your emotional, spiritual, and physical needs. They're all about your knowledge of connection, closeness, attachment, and aliveness. They infuse your mom presence with a felt sense of what it is to be dependent on others for care. Having your finger on the pulse of this kind of vulnerability is what helps you relate to your child with empathy. Where would moms be without empathy?

The Inner Baby is central to our work with moms. Knowing you have your own little one inside of you whom you must also pay attention to is a game changer. Don't get caught up in the semantics of the word "baby"—you can think of it as your inner child, or as very specific young parts of you. We use the word "baby" to try to capture the essence of your peak vulnerability and dependency—because we know it's the energy from that very fragile time in life that shapes our parts going forward. Those parts are the ones who show up in

INNER BABY PARTS

- Sad
- Scared
- Wanting

motherhood, with all kinds of ideas and beliefs and worries and hopes about what it is to be small.

Because they're exquisitely sensitive, Inner Baby parts are prone to shame. They're young (hence the name "baby"), and like all little ones, they automatically identify as the *cause* of the good things and the bad things that happen to them. Big, painful feelings like sadness and fear can easily open up the Inner Baby's treasure chest of historical shame, loading Mom's body with a sense of being somehow bad or broken or to blame.

When Inner Baby parts are outside of your awareness, unidentified and disowned, they create some serious complications. They distort your perspective and make you prone to unconscious projections that color and warp the way you see your kids. Yes, you're looking at your child, taking in the present-day scene, hearing what your kid is saying—but it's often through the eyes of your own sad, scared, hungry Inner Baby that you're seeing and feeling them. In large part, it's your own Inner Baby's tenderness that you feel when you engage with your children.

When Your Inner Baby Takes the Lead: Common Patterns

Mistaking your Inner Baby parts for your child's experience can be really helpful for creating empathic resonance. Inner Baby parts help you stand in your kid's shoes and feel more deeply into what's happening for them now. But your protectors have no clue that your own

Inner Baby's Sad, Scared, and Wanting parts are the fuel that's really driving them. They believe they're here protecting your child. And that can make them both self-righteous and hardheaded.

Once you become aware that you have your own Inner Baby who is informed by your childhood experience, you can start to see how you're borrowing from your past and bringing your unmet needs, fantasies, expectations, and assumptions into your mothering. You have more insight into how your projections are super helpful in certain moments and possibly harmful in others.

KENDRA'S STORY

Kendra has a young teenage daughter who participates in track and field at school and gets a lot of recognition from her peers for being fast and for winning. Kendra finds herself riding her daughter's highs with her, noticing a part that feels so much hope and pride in her girl's accomplishments, almost like they are her own. As she reflects, she shares:

"I never got to be part of anything in school. I lived with my grandma and she needed me to come home and do chores, and she got mad at me and was super judgmental if I was interested in normal teenage stuff. It feels like there's a big vacancy, a big hole in my life in this teenage part, who is still wanting to be accepted and who still wants the right jeans and to try out a bunch of different lip glosses. I have another part that's embarrassed to be fifty years old and still wishing I was a teenager. When my daughter does well or starts to seem popular, my own teen part gets so anxious and hopeful and even kind of jealous. I hate that I'm jealous of my own daughter. I find myself snapping at her and feeling kind of pissed off—because she's having such a good life."

As Kendra paused and went inside to be with her parts, she identified her Wanting, Resentful, and Anxious parts, noticing how they merged together and pulsed with jealousy. As she gave these parts more attention, she started describing a sense of emptiness and longing that her parts were pointing to. She could feel her own desire for connection with others and a need to belong that had been missing and aching all her life. With more courage and clarity, she was able to separate her experience from her daughter's, and when given some prompts to tell her parts' Truth, she said:

"I'm not getting my own needs met. And…it's not fair."

The tears arrived as she became more conscious of her own vulnerability and pain, and Kendra started to feel compassion for her teenage part who didn't get to be a teen. She saw how she had been feeling irritated with and resentful of her daughter for being happy and fulfilled in ways that her own Inner Baby was still hoping for. As the compassion came, so did her grief, which she said felt right, although it sparked some shame for how she's been chasing her childhood needs through her daughter. Kendra brought her compassion a little closer to her shame and was surprised by her ability to share such tender material so easily. We called this courage, and Kendra closed her eyes, feeling some new respect for herself. In the weeks that followed, instead of feeling resentful when her daughter shared good news, Kendra could recognize her Wanting part and speak to it with compassion: "I see you, Wanting part. You deserved to have those experiences too." This self-awareness allowed her to genuinely celebrate her daughter's achievements while also grieving her own losses.

Your Inner Baby holds your body's stored wisdom. But that wisdom is contextual and has to do with how you grew up. Because your Inner Baby is a baby—or a child—that means it's stuck in the past, still believing you're just as dependent on others' care and approval as you were in childhood. Your survival depended on receiving love, belonging, and acceptance when you were little, and your Inner Baby likely hasn't gotten the memo that things are different now. A couple of decades have passed, and you no longer need what you needed back then. Inner Baby parts often mistake motherhood as an opportunity to get their own needs met. Here are some troublesome Inner Baby dynamics that commonly show up in most of us:

Dynamic 1: You Expect Your Child to Make You Feel Better

Your protectors see your child as an opportunity to redo your Inner Baby's early experience and a chance to fix all the things that went wrong and to clean up old messes. And while there's validity to that perceived opportunity for healing, our kids aren't equipped to fulfill our dreams or heal our wounds for us. We want our kids' cooperation, respect, affection, and success—and our children are wildly unique people with their own needs, interests, destinies, struggles, and afflictions. Neurodivergence, developmental delays, illnesses, and personality quirks can get in the way of your kid becoming who you thought they would be or who you wanted them to be. Your Inner Baby was hoping you'd get some external validation from producing or raising a "normal" child or maybe an extraordinary child, and lo and behold, you got this one. As you witness your child's challenges, you're left with a sinking feeling that your child's struggle is evidence that as a mom, you're not quite *good enough*. And now everyone can see it confirmed.

In response to that feeling of not being *good enough*, you may step on the gas even harder, sacrificing more self-care, putting more time, energy, money, and urgency into your kids, steering with all your might in the direction of getting it just right and not missing anything. You enroll your kid in the right classes, get them tutoring and therapy, throw the amazing birthday parties, make the favorite dinner, chaperone the field trip, take the perfect family photos, and make sure you attend every single game or performance, shaping and pruning them (maybe raging at them in moments), all the while tracking yourself in comparison to all the other moms who seem to be killing it. And it starts to feel like your child is a project, and the success of the project is what will determine your worth, and so your kid better get their act together. This child was supposed to make you feel better and instead you're just tired.

Dynamic 2: You Do Everything for Your Child That You Wish Someone Had Done for You

Moms commonly travel with one of two wishes: "I'm going to give my child a childhood just like mine, and they're going to appreciate it and thrive," or "I'm going to make sure my child doesn't have a childhood anything like mine, and they're going to appreciate it and thrive." Both are setups for feelings of disappointment and failure. When you're determined to hit very specific motherhood-marks, you're positioned for pain when and if your efforts don't yield the intended results. Your wishes are well meaning but can entirely miss who your child really is—and the needs they have that are different from your own. It's helpful to realize that your Inner Baby has a story, and it isn't the same as your child's. When you are unconsciously trying to meet your needs through your child, you end up with two unhappy customers.

The question becomes, Is this about you or is this about your child? Kids want your attention to actually be on them (crazy, huh?). They do not want to be earmarked and appropriated for your unmet needs, your unfulfilled dreams, your wishes, and your anxiety. Kids are amazing bullshit detectors, even when they don't try to be. They just intuitively know when your parts are seeking fulfillment or soothing through their performance or behavior. Kids know when it's not actually their well-being you are attending to—it's your own hunger or your own discomfort. They'll feel this as pressure from you to be something other than what they are, and that creates fear and shame.

Dynamic 3: You Think You Have Control over Who Your Child Is and Who They Become

And because you have this persistent fantasy that you have control, you also believe that all the struggle and the suffering that you and your children feel are your own damn fault. You probably aren't a good mom. You should try harder.

It's really important to hear this:

> ✳ With motherhood, there are all kinds of things that we ultimately have zero control over. Influence? Yeah, some. Control? No.

Motherhood is, to some degree, disappointing. It's not what you expected or hoped for. And the truth is, regardless of how good a mom you are/were, it was going to be that way. Your kids were going to be who THEY are—not who you wanted them to be or who you raised them to be. We know, we know—it seems like some people have perfect kids and get exactly the mothering outcome they were hoping for, and it's true that there are instances where things line up really beautifully between a mom and her child. Well-suited temperaments, good timing, sufficient resources, fewer legacy burdens...Let's be glad for them. The world needs some well-adjusted, easygoing participants and contributors. But most of us are having a very human experience that includes a fair amount of struggle and suffering.

When we accept that we have no control over so much of this motherhood territory, we can start to be more honest about how it all feels. We can entertain words like "disappointment" and "longing" as we describe the truth of our experience. And what naturally follows is grief and sometimes shame, two states of being that moms work hard to avoid. When we understand ourselves as having many different parts, we have permission to feel many different ways all at once. It becomes possible to maintain love and morality even while we welcome our parts that had big expectations and have been disappointed by motherhood. We are able to orient with new openness and care to our grief and shame, and this creates space for new possibilities. And our kids are mightily relieved when we grant them the space to be who they truly are.

Dynamic 4: You Think Your Mistakes Are Unforgivable and Irreparable

Your Inner Baby and your protector parts see things in black and white and, in hard times, will incline you toward thinking you're a bad person who does bad things, period. Our young parts are undeveloped and can get locked in a mindset that leaves no room for hope. If your parts see you as someone unworthy of forgiveness, they may have decided you've made your bad-mom bed and now you must lie in it. Your parts don't know that you're an adult now, with the authority and power to repair mistakes, apologize authentically, and lean into inherent human resilience. Kid parts aren't sophisticated enough to see the big picture. They don't know humans are designed for this messy ride and that kids and adults alike can heal.

Wounded Inner Baby parts remember how it felt to get hurt. When they witness our mothering as being hurtful to our children, they flinch hard, and a whole slew of concerned protectors come rushing in to try to help. It's those "helpful" protectors who see our mistakes as unforgivable. It's our own parts that condemn us. And those parts need help rediscovering hope.

When we're caught in this cycle of self-condemnation, we often become desperate to prove we're not the terrible mothers our parts fear we are. We want to scrub the stains from our worn-out, beat-up vulnerability and make ourselves emerge capable and calm, worthy and lovable. And we inadvertently use our kids to attempt to springboard ourselves out of whatever inadequacy or insufficiency we're mired in and into a better story. If our kids can just grow and thrive and love and respect us, we can all get our needs met and emerge victorious!

Only, kids rarely want to play the part we've assigned them; they more often insist on being their random selves—sometimes occupying a completely noncomplementary role in our lives that only shines more light on how we are...failing. And that sense of failure can feel damning to our Inner Baby.

JOURNAL

Which wish did you come into motherhood holding?

- *I'm going to give my kid a childhood just like mine, and they're going to appreciate it and thrive.*
- *I'm going to make sure my kid doesn't have a childhood anything like mine, and they're going to appreciate it and thrive.*

Which of your parts drives the mission to be or not to be like your own mother? What is that part most afraid would happen if it stopped working so hard?

✳ You are not your child. Your child is not you. Both of you deserve to get the care you need.

Your kids need your curiosity. They want your fresh eyes and open heart to take in what they're feeling, thinking, and needing—separate from your own story. As you behold your child having a different life than you, your parts can be invited to gather round and take in the news. And sometimes it's really good news.

When Your Past Meets Your Child's Present

Your Inner Baby is the nexus at which your past meets your child's present. At that nexus, you are connected with all the love and all the wounding of your lineage. It's alive in you, coming up for consultation in your heart and mind now. You have an opportunity to bask in or drown in the legacies that are resurfacing. Recognizing the existence of your own Inner Baby gives you an access point so that you can edit and add to that legacy with consciousness and kindness.

Moms don't intend to project their unfinished business and unmet needs onto their children. It just happens. How could it go any differently? We arrive in motherhood with baggage. It's not a crime to have a trauma history or protector parts. In fact, you deserve to continue using your life for your own growth and benefit, even after you become a mom. Your Inner Baby and her unmet needs and burdened beliefs cannot help but emerge and overlay themselves upon your child, inviting your attention.

When we carry childhood wounds related to our essential worth, those wounds come up for review over and over again in motherhood. As we attempt to meet our children's needs and wants, our protector parts spot an opening for meeting our own. *Maybe if I can get my child to eat healthy foods, I'll get this thing with food right once and for all*—from a mom who struggled with an eating disorder all through adolescence. *By never making my son sleep alone and keeping him from ever having to feel terrified in the night like I did, I'll never have to feel those scary monster-under-the-bed feelings again*—from a mom who was deeply affected by nighttime neglect. *If my kid can get good grades and go to college, it will help take away some of the shame I feel about never graduating from high school*—from a mom who dropped out in her senior year because she had a baby. *I'll never let anyone speak to my child the way my dad spoke to me; if that means pulling my kid from public school and homeschooling, then so be it*—from a mom who vowed to make sure her child never felt belittled in the way she did when she was young. Our protectors double down on meeting our children's needs in the hope that they will simultaneously help our kids AND help address some unfinished business in our own emotional past.

When that happens, embrace the chance to see your parts more clearly. Take this as an opportunity to introduce your Inner Baby to your Inner Mom. We know that's easier said than done, but relief comes with just beginning to recognize the presence of your Inner Baby.

The tone of your early years taught you what it means to be vulnerable and dependent. Even if your parents were magnificent and you had a wonderful childhood, there were bumps in the road somewhere...

Powerlessness in infancy.

Shame from toddlerhood.

Rejection as an adolescent.

If you were hurt, abandoned, or sexually abused, those injuries will surface again in you when your child reaches the developmental stage at which you were wounded. It's good to know this in advance so that you can be prepared to care for yourself as you reencounter what was so painful or scary in your youth. Your Inner Baby needs a mother, and the best mother for her is you.

✳ One of the hardest things about motherhood is that moms are forced to feel their own childhood wounds once again. The beautiful thing is that moms get a chance to heal those wounds, with more resources and adult energy present.

Your Inner Mom

Meet your Inner Mom:

When the perinatal portal opens, mothers gain access to not just their Inner Baby, but also what we call the "Inner Mom." The Inner Mom is the term we use for the IFS concept of Self—the innate healing wisdom and capacity that exists without exception in all human beings, regardless of their trauma history or life circumstances. In our work with moms, we discovered that calling Self the "Inner Mom"

YOUR INNER MOM

A nurturing **internal resource** AND a highly developed **skill set** Mom can harvest for tending to her own Inner Baby.

A trustworthy source of internal care and nurturing that includes:
- New confidence about tending to distress
- More patience
- Access to a reservoir of unconditional love
- A new identity as a safe haven to someone else

Same as Self: curiosity, calmness, connectedness, choice, compassion, confidence, courage, creativity, and clarity

---

seemed to land better with our mom clients. Sometimes "Self" feels like an esoteric concept that's hard for people to grasp. But moms recognize this energy because they've accessed it while caring for their children—in moments when they instinctively knew how to comfort, when patience appeared out of nowhere, or when they felt deeply connected and present. We think of the Inner Mom like we think of Self-energy: relational, comforting, and understanding. Both seem to emanate connectedness, calmness, compassion, courage, and other healing qualities.

The Inner Mom isn't about being naturally "good" at mothering or having all the "right" feelings. It's also not the same as "maternal instinct," a concept that can feel like a setup for more feelings of inadequacy and failure as we wrestle with parts of us that *don't* like motherhood, that didn't instantly bond with our kids, and that feel completely fed up with the whole arrangement. Whether our parts took easily to motherhood or not has nothing to do with our Inner Mom or with our ability to lean into this concept. The Inner Mom is your capacity for presence, wisdom, and care—qualities that emerge naturally when your parts relax and trust that you can handle what's in front of you.

This is the beautiful paradox of motherhood: In learning to care for someone else's vulnerability, we develop exactly what we need to be with our own. Becoming a mother pushes us to learn a new set of skills for tending to vulnerability with consistency and care. Most of those precious resources get channeled directly into our emotionally ravenous children. But those same maternal resources can be used just as generously to care for our own Inner Baby.

You can include your Inner Baby in your daily mothering: When you feed your outer child, check and see if your Inner Baby is hungry too. When you hold your little one, see if your Inner Baby can be included in the hug. When you take a late-night call from your distraught adult child who tearfully shares that they're getting a divorce, notice how your own Inner Baby is feeling and let that matter to you. Anytime you're really activated or triggered as you relate to your kids, it's a good sign that your Inner Baby is HERE and needs attention.

You are mothering more babies than you think. Add up your kids and then add one more to that number—that's how many babies you're actually mothering. You need to differentiate yourself from your child so that you can meet both of your separate—and often conflicting—needs.

✴ Moms are always tending to two babies: one that lives outside and one that lives inside of them.

Motherhood is a unique and exciting opportunity to reach into the most vulnerable parts of ourselves and finally give them what they have been needing: attuned, responsive care. Inner Babies require compassionate attention and advocacy. Neglecting your Inner Baby moves you closer to your breaking point and perpetuates the handing down of family trauma. Thank goodness you have an Inner Mom.

Shifting Your Focus

You've been working hard at being a good mom to your children. You struggle at times, your kids throw you curveballs, and you try to course-correct, taking in new ideas and information about how you might dial it in better. You've read parenting books, listened to experts, absorbed the opinions of teachers and coaches. The world has lots of opinions and advice about how to be a better mom, and you take it all in. Of course, your friends and family weigh in too—and you listen to many, you ignore some, you integrate, you try new approaches, and you persevere in your effort to meet your kids' needs and support them through whatever phase of life they're in. You're freaking amazing. And likely very hard on yourself. And probably pretty tired.

This book isn't about mothering your kids. It's about mothering yourself. We're asking you to take all the juiciness you've extracted on your motherhood journey and start sharing it with yourself. We're giving you a way of seeing your internal world in simple terms (parts) so that you can begin responding to your pain and get to feeling better. It starts with knowing that you have your own Inner Baby who is hungry, scared, crying, lonely, wanting to play, and so on, existing right alongside your real-life child who is also making noise. Your Inner Baby has probably been ignored or neglected for a long time. No one sees, knows, or feels her the way that you do. Only you can really help her. Her unmet needs are the cause of much of your distress. And the wonderful news is you can bring your Inner Baby immediate relief. You can be her mom.

KELLY'S STORY

Kelly has no history with self-compassion. As a mother of three, she lives with the voice of her parents still ruling her inner world, reminding her that she's too anxious, too loud, too needy, too hungry. Her own Inner Critic shuts her up quickly when she senses she's too much now for anyone in her social circle or work world. She feels "at the mercy of other people" and imagines negative judgment coming from others, even when it's not there. "I'm too much" is the mantra of her parts, who feel a combination of anxiety and self-hate. Kelly identified her protectors as an Inner Critic, Destroyer, and Self-doubt.

Having worked with Kelly for several years now, I (Jessica) know her to be a loving and attentive mother. I asked her if she's ever been with one of her children when they were feeling some of these same kinds of feelings she suffers with—not good enough or like they're too much. She recalled lying in bed with a sad preteen daughter who just cried and cried while Kelly held her. Kelly recognized in the moment that she wasn't saying or doing much—just staying present with her daughter's big feelings and making it known that she was understood and she wasn't alone. She helped her daughter feel safe in a way that Kelly herself had never felt safe.

Kelly connected with the grief of her young self who felt entirely alone and had no one to comfort her in her own painful times. I asked her to locate in her body now the compassion and calm that flowed so beautifully toward her daughter and see if she could give it to her own Inner Baby. She was able to easily tap into her Inner Mom, through locating it in her role as a mother, and surprised herself when she realized how much care was available to her inside her own being. For the first time, she was able to bring a magnificent resource to her lonely Inner Baby.

✳ You can't give something to your child that you don't have for yourself. You *can* give yourself the good care you give to your child.

Many of us do not arrive in adulthood with healthy ways of listening to and caring for ourselves. We don't know we have parts. We don't accept or embrace our vulnerability. We care for ourselves the way we were cared for in childhood, or the way we have learned adaptively to survive, which isn't always kind or healthy. But motherhood grants us a bright, new awareness of how to attend to distress in a small, fragile creature. We learn how much it matters, and we learn how empowered we are to help. We learn that we have some or all of what it takes to be present with our child's vulnerability. We discover new capacities in ourselves and that we are psychologically bigger than the little beings whose dependency we hold. Coming to trust our psychological strength and capacity is reflective of the trust we develop in ourselves as moms. Now we can use that knowledge and that new skill set to be present with our own fragility too. Our Inner Mom can become a safe haven not only for our child, but also for ourselves.

A Meditation for Mothering Your Inner Baby

Go inside and see if you can connect with the way you feel when you are most Irritated with or Anxious about your child. Take a moment to let a memory resurface so that you can really feel yourself get triggered. As that activation shows up in your body, notice how it feels. What is it doing to your muscles? To your face? To your breathing? How does it make your voice sound when you speak to your child? How does your child react to this part of you?

As you start to pay attention to it, notice the thoughts this part is thinking: What is it worried about? What's it remembering from your past? How old were you when that happened? Who took care of you then? Did you get the care you needed?

How are you feeling toward this part as you learn more about its wounds? This is your Inner Baby, or one of your Inner Babies, and she's here, hoping for some attention. Here are some healing ideas you can share with her:

- Let her know that she is no longer powerless. She has you here. You can speak for her, take action, clarify her boundaries—things she couldn't do when your body was little.
- Show her that you realize she's just a child, doing the best she knows how to do. Let her know you aren't ashamed of her (if that's authentic).
- Hold her. It's less lonely when you have someone who can hold you.
- Show her how she never lost you and she can never lose you. Let her know you really understand her in a way that nobody else ever will—because you were there through her whole childhood. And you will be here for the rest of her life.

It's you whom she needs now; no one else can meet her needs in the same way. No one else has shared her experience. You know exactly what kind of care and mothering she needs. She can tell you in ways that only you understand. How does it feel to get to know your Inner Baby, and to treat her with kindness and respect?

IFS offers a model for healing these young parts of yourself—bringing them out of the past and updating them with the good news that you're an adult now with access to resources. These parts have felt powerless. You are now able to address your needs directly from a calm, centered place and then make an adult decision about how you want to show up in your relationships, ask for what you need, and take in the goodness that's here for you.

You were very small once. You received a particular quality of care that shaped your sense of yourself, your beliefs about other people, and your perception of the world around you.

JOURNAL

What was your early experience of being dependent and vulnerable like? Were you safe? Did you feel loved and cared for? Or were you in danger, subjected to neglect or abuse? When you think about needing care from other people, what happens inside you?

The Wisdom in the Wound

Moms very often confuse their Inner Baby for their present-day baby or child. Because moms' Inner Baby blends with their real-life kid, moms struggle to see the difference between their own pain and their child's pain. Where there are really two separate vulnerable beings, Mom just sees one. She cares for her outer baby/kid the way her Inner Baby tells her to, not realizing when she's missing the mark for both. She thinks she's acting in service of her child, when, in fact, her own parts have unmet needs and a pressing agenda for love, connection, or redemption that are trying to be satisfied.

Your Inner Baby will always be here, helping clue you in to your child's experience but also reminding you of your own needs and wants—and your own unfinished emotional business. With practice and patience, you can start to tune in to your Inner Baby's wounds and unmet needs and pause to take care of yourself. Though it's not possible to go back and redo your childhood, your parts that were hurt in the past can be cared for today. A tremendous amount of healing comes from loving ourselves through motherhood and then witnessing the gift of our healing as it's shared with our children.

Chapter 4

Why Moms Have Mom Parts

Babies and children require a ridiculous amount of care and attention—
there's just no getting around it. Along with getting their basic physical needs met, our little ones need to feel loved and respected too.
The security of the connection that we offer our kids and the culture
we create within our relationship matter more than we realize. How
we talk to them, how we respond to their expressions, and how we
feel about mothering them—this is all communicated to our kids and
internalized by them in ways that shape their health for the entirety of
their lives.

Motherhood is a long, complex, and high-stakes journey that calls
upon us to lead dependent, vulnerable, wildly reactive, less-developed
human beings through mundane as well as extraordinary life experiences. Our goals are complicated and weighty: keeping our children
safe, supporting them in becoming contributing members of society,
actualizing their talents, and developing rich, meaningful relationships. Not small potatoes.

The weight of this responsibility exacts a heavy emotional toll
on many mothers—a heaviness that's often amplified by living in a
culture that provides inadequate support for this monumental task.
We're expected to manage this complex work with minimal resources
and little help, often in isolation. Most mothers are doing the hardest job in the world without the village, without adequate childcare,

without paid family leave, and often without partners who share the load equally.

So much about our kids' wellness is riding on our mothering.

(PRESSURE.)

How we mother our kids shapes their nervous systems.

(PRESSURE.)

The responsibility is enormous.

(PRESSURE!)

Your anxiety, your rage, your impatience, your trauma history, and your sadness all deeply affect them.

(PRESSURE!!)

What does it mean about me if my kid is struggling? How do I not blame myself if my child is failing? Or what if my baby is born with a genetic disorder or congenital anomaly? Or has trouble reading? Or is antisocial or just…rude? Or gets into drugs? If my teen develops an eating disorder, it must be my fault. What do I do if my child is othered by society and becomes a target for cruelty and hate? It's my job to make sure they stay safe. And it's also my job to make sure they become the best version of themselves. If anything goes wrong, it's…my fault.

(OMG—SO MUCH PRESSURE!!)

The takeaway is this: Any mistake you make could be the cause of your child's failure to thrive; therefore, you need to do everything exactly right and be a perfect mother. Bring on the hardworking Mom Parts!

Meanwhile, we're bombarded with curated images of perfect motherhood on social media—aggressively aesthetic birthday parties, organic homemade meals, and professionally zen mothers who seem to have it all figured out. We compare our messy reality to these impossible standards while navigating judgment from other moms who are likely struggling just as much but presenting a publicly polished facade. *Ugh.*

Cue our internal backup team. When we're this overwhelmed and underresourced, our protector parts naturally activate to help us cope with and manage the relentless demands that modern motherhood presents us with.

Understanding Your Internal World

Protector parts show up automatically when they determine we need them, just as our heart beats when it receives the signal to pump blood. These parts are as real and integral to us as our organs—we can't remove them and wouldn't want to. They're functional components of our psyche with particular roles to play. The challenge is that parts often run on autopilot, and we blend with them without realizing it, failing to recognize when their narrow focus has taken over our broader perspective.

Protector parts are devoted to our well-being, and their actions were, at one point in time, critical to our belonging and our survival. Knowing that every one of our parts has good intentions gives us freedom and courage to approach them with curiosity. Our genuine interest coaxes them out of reflexive, unconscious reactivity and invites a new internal conversation. We start to make friends with each other.

Having awareness of ourselves as multiple minds and being able to identify parts and how they activate inside of us give us a powerful new tool for calming internal chaos and finding inner balance.

CARRIE'S STORY

Carrie went back to work when her daughter was six months old. She initially felt lucky to be able to take a full six months off work, recognizing that many of her peers had to return within weeks of giving birth, due to financial need or employer inflexibility. Carrie loved her job before she got pregnant and identified as a type A person who prided herself on being self-reliant, focused, and successful. But after a challenging birth experience and a slow recovery, Carrie found herself in a very different frame of mind, feeling sad and tired and like she just wanted to stay home with her little girl.

"I don't fit into my work clothes, and I just don't feel like being a salesperson anymore. I'm lost. I'm not my old self, but I'm also kind of sad and bored just being a mom," she shared tearfully.

Every day she pulled up to work in tears, struggling to get out of her car and put on her "professional game face" after dropping her baby off at day care. "The day care provider is super sweet, but my baby looks so sad when I leave, and I can hear her crying when I walk out the door. I feel like a terrible mom. I mean, how is my job more important than my daughter? It fucking sucks to have to choose—and to be choosing work over her!"

When Carrie had a chance to receive support in therapy and start sorting through her Mom Parts, she went inside and connected with her Caretaker part, who was really pissed at her Responsible and Superwoman parts, who thought they would have no trouble going back to work. Those hardcore manager parts expected her to jump right back in after giving birth, without missing a beat. Her Caretaker part felt like she was being ripped away from her baby, which was stirring up uncomfortable thoughts and stories in her Anxious part.

Exploring the fears of these polarized parts who felt so at war inside of her helped Carrie put words to the chaotic feelings that had been overwhelming her. Carrie's struggle became less about her being a bad mom/employee and more about being in the throes of a very challenging time of life. With increased clarity, Carrie felt more empowered when she decided she wanted to speak to her boss about reducing her hours. When she approached her supervisor, she was able to speak from her Inner Mom rather than her desperate parts: "I'd like to explore options for working part-time for the next six months while I adjust to being a new mom." Her clear, nonreactive approach led to a conversation about flexible arrangements that worked for everyone.

Carrie's experience illustrates something crucial: Being able to identify your parts is a superpower. Rather than seeing your Anxiety and Guilt as just unwanted or problematic emotions that you wish you didn't have, you can begin to understand that your parts are here to try to help you—even when they wind up hurting you. This kind of internal listening creates a pause where curiosity and compassion can show up early, preventing the reaching of painful breaking points.

Understanding how your parts relate to each other is equally important. Some parts work together harmoniously—they complement each other and agree on a common mission. For example, Caretaker and Mama Bear parts often have very compatible interests and concerns. Other parts feel completely in opposition to each other, holding an attitude of win or lose, all or nothing. These polarized parts create internal wars that push moms to their breaking point, where other parts take over and launch moms into patterns of lashing out, collapsing, disconnecting, or self-medicating. Carrie's Responsible, Superwoman, and Caretaker parts were locked in exactly this kind of battle—one group of parts insisting she could handle everything; the other feeling concerned that she was abandoning her baby.

These internal conflicts are often intensified by the cultural messages we've absorbed about what it means to be a good mom—messages that create additional polarizations within us.

✳ You have parts with very different agendas—parts dedicated to caring for your child and parts that remember who you are, separate from being a mom—and this creates internal conflict.

The Taboo of Wanting (Anything Besides Motherhood)

In our patriarchal culture, the only needs and wants that are accepted and endorsed in motherhood are those that pertain directly to motherhood, to your children, and to the actualization of yourself as a mother. For many women, this kind of needing and wanting is real and authentic: The pursuit of motherhood, the aching for it, the joy that it brings, and the self-trust and the healing that it engenders are found to be among the richest, most fulfilling, heart-expansive experiences that exist.

But what about wanting attention, connection, art, sensuality, acclaim, eroticism, accolades, power, autonomy, expression, alone time, or any other kind of wanting that is distinct from motherhood? That stuff is all morally suspect and selfish and is frowned upon in women, most especially in mothers. That kind of Wanting gets shamed, silenced, and inhibited—definitely not respected or inquired into.

This taboo fractures us internally. When whole aspects of our humanity become unacceptable, we develop parts that hide these needs and other parts that police them relentlessly. Your Good Mom parts do their best to push your Inner Baby and all her big, messy feelings into dormancy. But you can only hit snooze on your wants and needs so many times. This internal split is a recipe for exactly the kind of polarized suffering that drives mothers to their breaking point.

An Inner Baby exists in all of us, and if that Inner Baby's wants and needs aren't given some space to be known and explored, it will sneak its way secretly and covertly up into and between your Mom Parts. It will croon mournfully about who you know yourself to be down deep, separate from your children.

✳ You have parts that know what you need and parts that silence those needs—and this internal conflict is normal and workable.

This Isn't What I Signed Up For

When motherhood doesn't meet our expectations, we understandably get distressed. We start feeling like there isn't a whole lot in the experience of motherhood that's actually FOR us. We kind of start to hate it. And then we feel guilty for being angry at our (helpless, dependent) kids. *What kind of mother am I? What's wrong with me?*

This creates another painful polarization: Our Bored and Irritated parts clash violently with our Fixer and Caretaker parts. The Bored part is craving new stimulation, and our Fixer part is horrified by our disinterest in dress-up games, *Minecraft* tutorials, and art projects with glitter everywhere. Our Inner Critic shows up to point out all the ways we're failing our kids, and the cacophony of parts starts to nudge us into self-doubting, self-hating territory where we catch a ride on the patriarchal wave and gaslight ourselves for our own unhappiness. *I'm a shit mom—that's why I'm unhappy.*

Feeling guilty and being angry are common, familiar experiences for moms. And while neither anger nor guilt are fun places to hang out, they're more comfortable than the deeper truth of disappointment that's likely there, underlying all that anger and guilt. Disappointment holds so much shame, grief, and loss—emotions our Good Mom parts simply cannot tolerate.

And disappointments abound in motherhood. As much as we love them, kids are not created to our specifications, nor are they necessarily a great match for our preferences and temperaments. They're just random people, packaged up by our bodies and/or delivered into our lives, with their own inclinations, afflictions, gifts, and destinies. They will surprise you and wow you and blow your mind, and they will scare you and disappoint you. They did not come equipped with what's needed to soothe or heal your unmet needs. And they suck up a lot of your time and energy.

You had an expectation, like so many new moms before you, that your good mothering would create loving kids who would complement your life, enhance your joy, and expand your heart on the regular. But the truth is your kid doesn't say thank you, doesn't eat the dinner you made, doesn't notice that you got them to practice on time again, or that you didn't sleep last night thanks to their intrusions. They don't reliably show affection or respect. Maybe they didn't get the good grades that would've affirmed your solid parenting and fabulous genes. Perhaps they didn't brush their teeth or go to class at all yesterday or choose a worthy boyfriend or girlfriend. They don't seem to notice that you cashed out your 401(k) to pay for their treatment. All the high-quality mothering you gave them did not, in fact, dismantle patriarchy, create peace in the world, or even create peace in your own home. And that's fucking disappointing.

For some crazy reason, most of us go into motherhood expecting just the opposite—expecting that our goodness and lovability will be reflected back to us through the adoring eyes of our kids. We will finally be discovered as worthy and valuable, healed of our long-standing sense of loneliness or not enoughness. We have fantasies that our good mothering will create healthy, kind, intelligent kids who contribute to society in ways that amplify our values and validate our deepest hope: that we are, in fact, good moms.

JOURNAL

Where have you felt disappointed by motherhood?

Are any parts of you uncomfortable with acknowledging your disappointment?

Is it possible to be disappointed **and** feel your uncomfortable parts at the same time?

What's it like to remind yourself that all Mom Parts have wisdom and need space to be explored.

When we're disappointed by motherhood or disappointed in our children, our Mom Parts freak out. The whole world's Mom Parts freak out! Kids aren't supposed to be disappointing, and moms aren't supposed to feel disappointed. There's a huge taboo around maternal disappointment, and that taboo makes it very difficult to speak the truth. Disappointment directed at our kids registers as a huge threat. Not liking the powerless people who are dependent on us reads as a moral betrayal to the parts of us who took an oath to protect and serve.

If you listen carefully to your Mom Parts, they will likely share that they're afraid that if you acknowledge any disappointment you feel about your kids or about motherhood, you are entering the territory of separateness, and if you're not careful, you might actually make a run for it and abandon those high-maintenance disappointments altogether. Or kill them. Disappointed moms are dangerous and shameful. Your kids wouldn't be disappointing if you had been a better mother. *It's your fault*, according to your Good Mom parts.

Disappointment's Detour

Rather than face the wrath of our parts who cannot stomach the thought of us being disappointed—of beholding our child as less than lovable or desirable, of wishing we had never become a mother—our protector parts find another solution. They shift the focus of our unhappiness away from our child and onto a different target. The problem needs to be addressed, but it needs to be located in someone other than the vulnerable child.

So we swallow it down with some acidic inner criticism and let it fester in our own dark interior (*I'm a bad mom*). Or we spew it out at our coworker or the guy driving like a maniac in the car passing us on the right, or better yet, our partner—who perhaps doesn't feel nearly as disappointed by parenthood as we do. Who's gonna take the hit? Where can all this sorrow and despair be directed?

And we've got other parts who register disappointment in motherhood and are happy to take over and look for a new source of dopamine by investing in a different fantasy. Extramarital affairs, workaholism, and plastic surgery are all viable options for fantasy incubation. Fantasy was a valid and lifesaving aspect of childhood that helped us expand beyond the limiting confines of our families of origin. We needed it to cultivate a vision of what was possible and to give our Inner Baby inspiration or hope. But as adults, fantasy can send us on a dry run in search of our Inner Baby's unmet needs that cannot be met in adulthood. We carry the belief from childhood that to be redeemed, we need approval, safety, love, and validation from an external source. But as adults, it isn't true. Our parts primarily need our own love and approval. Nobody else can actually meet your Inner Baby's needs now. Hold your Inner Baby close while you read this: *Sweetheart, that ship has sailed.*

✷ Your unmet needs from childhood cannot be met by anyone other than you—not your children, not your partner, not your next promotion or affair.

MARGO'S STORY

Margo is mom to a teenage daughter who's going away to an out-of-state college in the fall on a volleyball scholarship. She sought out therapy to explore the feelings coming up around being an empty nester and having more space to herself for the first time in nearly two decades. Margo is a self-described "helicopter mom" whose life has revolved around her star athlete for years on end. She described herself feeling "blue and out of sorts" as she attempted to navigate the space opening up in her life and seeing her beloved daughter off.

"I'm so proud of her, but I also feel disappointed. I put everything I had into her—and now she's taking it and leaving. I always knew she'd grow up, but in some way, I'm feeling abandoned. I've been busy focusing on her and resenting my husband for so many years now, I don't really know what to do with the years ahead."

Margo spent time in therapy exploring the ins and outs of hanging on loosely while learning to let go. As she identified her Caretaker and Resentful parts, she was able to speak a truth she'd been avoiding—that for a very long time, she'd been ignoring her own needs, and she was scared to look closely at what she might find.

A few months later, with her daughter thriving at college, Margo joined a hiking group and started training for a half-marathon. "I realized my Caretaker part had been so focused on orchestrating my daughter's success that I'd forgotten about my own body and what it could do," she shared. The empty nest that had meant irrelevance began to feel like an invitation to inhabit her own life fully again.

When Protection Creates Disconnection

As long as our Good Mom parts are able to keep doing their jobs—controlling, putting out fires, fixing problems, meeting needs, being patient, pushing their improvement agendas, and pleasing others—the system holds steady. We may have an autoimmune disease or a secret drinking habit or a miserable marriage, but we're still momming effectively, dammit. We are consumed with the enormous job of protecting what's vulnerable, but the soul of our lives—the soul of motherhood—gets lost in the process.

Protector parts all share some common features: They're developmentally young, they're driven by fear, they operate on procedural memory (automatic pilot), and they have an agenda. Since fear is a common denominator for all protectors, they're focused on their mission of trying to keep you safe and having your needs met. Being young and unsophisticated, they lack the developmental capacity to hold conflicting truths simultaneously, and they tend to split the world into simplified absolutes that are very black and white.

Because our protectors are so fear-based and mission-driven, they narrow our focus and channel our energy in targeted ways that keep us from being open, relaxed, flexible, or curious. Hoping to protect us, they inadvertently make us more rigid and isolated. It's sad but true that our protectors seem to create the very situations they're trying so hard to help us avoid. They want safety and love, but they blow it through their misguided efforts.

Humans operate in either connection mode or protection mode. You can't be open and closed at the same time. If one of your protectors is feeling activated and has taken the wheel, you effectively close down and enter into protection mode. The people around you won't find you easy to connect with. To shift back into connection mode, your protector parts have to register that it's safe to do so.

✳ Humans operate in either connection mode or protection mode. You can't be open and closed at the same time.

The Burdens We Carry

While all protectors are motivated by fear, some of our protectors are burdened by what IFS refers to as extreme beliefs, emotions, and energies that completely color their behavior and reactions.[1] If we endured abuse or neglect in our formative years, our parts will be weighed down by painful emotional burdens.

Parts also carry burdens handed down through our larger family lineage by ancestors who endured traumatic events in the distant or not-so-distant past. When our families carry histories of persecution, war, racism, starvation, torture, death, or abandonment, those memories travel through time. Our ancestors' protector parts pass the painful stories down to us, hoping to keep us safe from the threats that existed in their era. With or without words, those tragedies are bequeathed to the next generation in the form of inherited trauma—or what IFS calls legacy burdens.

We all have parts that carry burdens. When our parts are burdened, they are forced to occupy certain protective roles within our system. Under duress, they figure out how they need to contort themselves and where they need to bring their muscle to help us make it through precarious situations. These parts tend to be frozen in historical time, continuing to do the important work they started back when we were little, never getting the memo that we're grown up now.

Your parts are very young. They're limited in their ability to see the big picture. They're scared. They view the world in black and white, and they split things into binary categories of good or bad. They don't feel authentically empowered or deeply resourced. They don't trust you. They're scrappy and a little overzealous. And like little children, they need care, validation, and support.

All of your parts have their own unique perspective and experience. The goal behind getting to know and understand your parts is that you can get some new perspective on them that will help you see them more clearly and have a little energy that's separate from their energy. Unblending from your parts helps dial down the intensity that they bring to your life. Separating from them a tiny bit helps them soften. They relax, and as they do so your relationship with your parts feels quite different. There's new curiosity and, over time, maybe even some affection. They start to trust you as an Inner Mom when you start treating them like legitimate beings who have valid feelings and needs. Having a connected relationship with your parts is a solid definition of good mental health.

Chapter 5

Meet Your Mom Parts

To kick off your relationship-building journey with your Mom Parts, we've mapped out these key players in the maternal system and given you some colorful bios for each part, fleshing out common fears and hopes that these kinds of parts are designed to navigate. And for each part, we've also offered some ideas about how you might start to experience and relate to them when you feel more compassion for them coming from your Inner Mom. It's true that as you spend time going inside and getting to know and appreciate your parts, your Inner Mom begins to occupy more square footage, setting a new tone of self-compassion or at least curiosity. Having an Inner Mom who is present with the parts of us who are struggling opens up more hope and choice inside of us.

These descriptions are intended to surprise you. We highlight some of the paradoxical intentions and behaviors that can help us get curious about parts we took for granted. Use these descriptions as a guide where they feel supportive and affirming of your experience. But in the event your experience does NOT match our descriptions, trust your intuition and insight. These descriptions are by no means comprehensive or completely accurate to everyone; your protectors may share some but not all of these attributes, so please feel free to take liberties with our words. As you read, keep in mind that regardless of the protector's name or how it's known in your system, the part originated to try to help you. Its aim was to take care of you.

ANGRY

Your Angry part loves you. It shows up to clarify when and where you've been disrespected and energizes your entire being, readying you for a fight. Your Angry part knows where your shame is hiding, and it's sworn to secrecy, focusing instead on grooming an attack dog who will bark and lunge at anyone who oversteps. The barking and lunging are designed to scare people off; all that ferocity gives your Angry part a bad reputation, but this protector is really a sensitive flower who wants more than anything to make sure you don't get hurt. Anger guards your tenderness and hidden shame with great care and devotion. When it witnesses you being misunderstood, disrespected, unseen, unvalued, or obstructed, the leash comes off the attack dog.

Fears: If I don't bite back, I won't be respected.

Hopes: If I scare them enough, I'll make sure that people treat me with more respect.

Your Inner Mom can help appreciate your Angry part's alerts about where you've felt hurt or disrespected without getting swept away by its energy. You'll remember that Anger is here to guard your shame, and you'll show it how your shame is a wound that you're working to heal. You'll learn how your Angry part felt powerless and bullied when you were small, and you'll update it now—showing it that you have more freedom and choice and that you can advocate for yourself from a place of internal steadiness and self-compassion. You'll pet Anger's dog and give it a treat for not barking and lunging.

ANXIOUS

Your Anxious part is designed to keep you and your dependents alive and well. It functions like a filter, identifying and avoiding potential threats to your loved ones (and there are soooo many of them when it comes to babies and children). Your Anxious part keeps your eyes scanning and your ears tuned for any sign of trouble, and it gets overloaded with motherhood's round-the-clock use. Other parts of you that crave more ease or feel judgmental about your level of vigilance will hate on your Anxious part, and all its accompanying adrenaline and cortisol that burn you out. When the overwhelmed protective filter becomes clogged, it needs care and restoring, not rejection—care that reaches the center of your nervous system and establishes S-A-F-E-T-Y. Anxious parts are often running on outdated or generationally inherited programming that hasn't been updated with information about your present-day resources and capacities. You have the power to give your Anxious part the update it's been waiting for.

Fears: If I stop being vigilant and bracing for danger, something terrible could happen to me or my child.

Hopes: Anticipating potential problems and threats will keep me calm (ha!) and keep my child safe.

Your Inner Mom can help you become friendlier with your Anxious part, beginning by offering appreciation for its years of tireless service. When your Anxious part starts to trust that it has your Inner Mom as an onboard ally, it will feel the kind of calm that comes with supportive partnership. Listen respectfully to your Anxious part's concern, but make sure it can feel you there listening, so that it notices there is a YOU present who honors its alarm without falling under its spell. Your Inner Mom can soothe your Anxious part, reminding it that it comes from a very long line of Anxious ancestors who had to outrun ferocious predators. They made it—and so did you! That is very good news. And . . . you are the heir to some mighty Anxious parts.

BLAMER

The Blamer feels shame and tries to help you off-load the bad feeling by projecting it outward onto someone else. It's obvious to this part that someone is in the wrong, and it doesn't want that someone to be you. The Blamer is a young child who sees the world in black and white. It has a lightning-quick reactive response when it's been perceived or portrayed as bad, guilty, or unlikable. Not yet knowing that it's safe to witness other people's disappointment without feeling at fault (or that it's safe to get to know your own shame), the Blamer is like an aggressive goalie who keeps kicking the ball back out of your goal. By continually lobbing it back at someone else, the Blamer unintentionally affirms the shame of your tender, wounded parts who really just want to be seen and held and forgiven by the one person whose opinion truly matters to them now: you. The Blamer may be aggressive and quick, but it's driven by fear and a lack of embodied empowerment. Every time the Blamer blames, it delays your own healing.

Fears: Maybe I'm the bad one.

Hopes: If it's someone else's fault, I won't have to feel exposed or ashamed.

Your Inner Mom can help you see how your Blamer is trying to spare you from shame. Your compassion will help it soften its tone and its attack, and instead give you access to its tender center. You'll take an interest in understanding the belief it's holding about your own badness, and you'll bring it the good news: You've been innocent in your heart all along. You'll show it how magnificent and empowering it is to be able to stay openhearted, even in moments that make you feel bad.

BORED

Your Bored part is especially sensitive to a lack of attunement from your environment. It's aware that your need for connection or stimulation is not being met, and it pops in, looking for some action. It starts flirting with your Wanting part, reminding you about your fantasies, your longing, and your unmet needs, and if it's ignored, your Bored part will reject the status quo and start stirring up some trouble by seeking external stimulation (perhaps of the bad-mom variety). Your Bored part doesn't know that you're empowered; it rebels against the perceived constraints of your deprivation and neglect, not realizing that you are now capable of attuning to yourself. You can strike the match that gets your fire started without burning the house down.

Fears: I can't get what I need here.

Hopes: If I get creative and go rogue, maybe I'll feel alive again.

Your Inner Mom can help bring your Bored part your own genuine curiosity. You can promise it that you won't let the flame of your desire and inspiration die. You'll find its spark and help light things up inside of you again—it just might not be this very instant. When your Bored part is respectfully acknowledged and supported by your Inner Mom, it deepens into patience.

CARETAKER

Your Caretaker part is a superhighway for TLC. It makes itself valuable, sometimes irreplaceable, by offering care and emotional attunement to the people who are important to us. The caretaker has deep faith in its own magic and can't imagine that there are limits to its capacity. Giving care can feel good and create connectedness in relationships, which motivates the Caretaker to keep up the "good" work and maintain the lovefest. The problem, if there is one, is that your Caretaker part is doing hard work that can bypass YOUR needs. If you were parentified as a very young child you learned how to fine-tune your caregiving skills in response to parents who needed you. Your Caretaker part exiled your vulnerability in order to stay focused on supporting Mom or Dad. The generous gifts that your Caretaker bestows on others are often self-sacrificial, and at some point, your Caretaker will probably hit a wall. It will run out of steam, which often manifests in physical depletion and illness. Your Caretaker is a nurturing part that can feel devastated by the reality of its limitations to make things better for everyone else.

Fears: If I'm not taking care of the people around me, those people will fall apart.

Hopes: If I take good care of others, they'll be happier and more available and loving toward me.

Your Inner Mom can help love and appreciate your Caretaker part for its intuitive clarity about others' needs and for all the delicious connection it creates in your relationships. You can hold it when it feels sad about its own limitations (you can't save everyone). You can help it rest and take a back seat so that you too can be the recipient of restorative, good care. You can start to inquire into your own unmet needs with genuine interest and new compassion.

CONTROLLER

Your Controller is wicked-smart. It has keen awareness about what needs to be done and the best way to do it. The thing is, it doesn't trust other people. It's been disappointed in the past when others have pretended to be capable leaders. So it does what it believes is necessary and starts using its elbows and its loud voice to wrestle everyone out of the way so it can take the wheel and steer to safety. Your Controller shoulders the burden of responsibility that goes with being in charge, and it burns your life force as its fuel, rendering you hungry, depleted, and edgy. Though its tight grip is often what saves the day, the Controller's tightness also keeps you from relaxing and from feeling open and present. It cuts you off from deeply connecting with others, and it creates tension in your close relationships.

Fears: Nobody else is capable or trustworthy. I'm not safe in others' hands.

Hopes: If I take on a little more responsibility and effort, I can hold things together.

Your Inner Mom can help you tap into trusting something greater than your own efforts to control the world around you. As your trust expands, your Controller can experiment with relaxing its tight grip, and it will likely start to grieve all that it has missed out on. Grief will help soften your Controller and allow it to be more receptive to love and support from outside, giving you access to greater ease, more connection, and new joy.

DEPRESSED

Your Depressed part knows you're wounded. It tourniquets the wound and cuts off circulation to save you from what feels like a life-threatening injury. This "lifesaving" measure succeeds in shutting off contact with the source of your pain, which keeps you alive but leaves you feeling numb, heavy, and disconnected from yourself. Like bystanders at a terrible accident, a whole host of concerned protector parts gather nearby, frightened by the wound and fretting about the tourniquet. Their agitation and despair create panic and confusion, causing the Depressed part to pull the tourniquet even tighter. Hopelessness spreads through your entire system.

Fears: It's not safe to feel what I feel.

Hopes: I'll be safer if I feel less.

Your Inner Mom can help you appreciate your Depressed part for how it's attempting to save you. She will move closer to this protective part and begin to identify the other voices in the concerned chorus: your Inner Critic's, along with any overtones belonging to Angry, Controller, or Destroyer parts. Your Inner Mom will gently coax each of the individual protectors away from the site of the wound so she can focus on tending to the injury. She may discover that your Depressed part has been carrying an enormous load, and she will help it release some of that burden. You will find there's more space now for your sadness and soulfulness to be invited back into your life. Relief gets redefined, not as escape from sorrow but as the inclusion of grief into your heart.

DESTROYER

Your Destroyer aims to take out your vulnerability so that no one else can. The Destroyer is acutely aware of your unmet needs and is convinced they are going to continue to be unmet. It cannot tolerate the humiliation of you feeling rejected, and it has absorbed the message that getting what you most want or need is not possible. Ever. It seemingly turns against YOU, like a kind of inner Fuck-it part, which can feel violent and destructive. In fact, the Destroyer is trying to help you stay empowered, and it does the one thing it knows how to do: destroy the vulnerable target (your own unmet needs). It wants nothing more than to keep exposure and humiliation to a minimum, so it looks to kill your soft spot before anyone else can.

Fears: I will be humiliated and robbed of power.

Hopes: I'll never get my needs met, but I can save a sliver of my integrity.

Your Inner Mom can help you recognize that the Destroyer shows up when you feel the most vulnerable, and you will be able to take it in your arms and offer it compassion. You will see your Destroyer part as a call to grieve much more honestly and completely: *You did not get what you needed when you needed it. It was humiliating and excruciating. You deserved good care.* Over time, as you demonstrate your interest in your own needs and vulnerability, the Destroyer will come to learn that it's no longer required in that big, destructive way. It will be able to soften and cry with you.

FIXER

Your Fixer part feels empowered and often mandated by necessity to deliver results. It's competent and relied upon, and it carries a heavy load in motherhood, solving problems and volunteering your body, mind, and creativity for more than your share of labor. Your Fixer earned you your great reputation for being the go-to person who handles every crisis, but because it leads by *doing*, it can miss out on being present, connected, and embodied. All that jumping in and *doing* can be depleting for your system, and it's also nonrelational. Your Fixer part tends to bypass others' capabilities and misses opportunities to let other people step up and figure things out for themselves. Fixers can get grumpy when others don't step up, and exhausted from carrying more than their share.

Fears: If I don't fix this, it will stay broken.

Hopes: If I get involved and take this on, I can rescue the situation and create a little peace for everyone.

Your Inner Mom can help shower your Fixer with gratitude for its amazing skill set. What a gift it is! You will also be able to take a breath before jumping in and assigning yourself the job of saving the day by looking around and seeing if someone else may be able to step in at times. You'll remember that as competent as your Fixer may be, exploiting it makes you feel separated and lonely. You'll take a deep breath and refrain from fixing, appreciating the courage it takes to allow things to be as they are.

FRUSTRATED

Your Frustrated part wants to make something happen that isn't happening. It can hear the voice of your Good Mom parts reminding you to *just breathe through this*, but it also hears the not-too-distant growl of your fury, tempting it to escalate. It settles for a grumpy tone or some mean-spirited words that make others want to keep their distance. Frustrated parts are frequent fliers in moms' worlds and hold the unique role of being one of the only socially acceptable expressions of maternal discontent. Your Frustrated part represents your legitimate anger without moving into territory that our culture deems morally suspect and threatening. So it makes itself comfortable in your life, taking up space in your head and in your thoughts and seeping into all your relationships.

Fears: If I stop trying, everyone will just ignore what needs to happen.

Hopes: If I put a little growl into this, maybe I can change it.

Your Inner Mom can help you soften toward your Frustrated part, whose dissatisfaction can color your daily life. You'll start to understand how your Frustrated part is afraid it's all alone and unsupported in the world. You'll hear how it feels like getting what you need is an uphill battle, and you'll start showing up as a friend instead of a critical or rejecting voice. "How can I help?" you'll ask it. When your Frustrated part is supported by your Inner Mom, it's known to burst into self-compassion.

FUCK-IT

Your Fuck-it part may feel like it has a lot of negative energy behind it, but this part really has your back and wants to help you get at least one or two of your unmet needs addressed. Fuck-it knows you are fed up, tired, exhausted, overwhelmed, and burned out, and it has noticed a couple of unacceptable trends in your life: People don't come through for you, and you also don't come through for yourself. It sees that you're stuck. Fuck-it grabs the keys out of your hand, takes its place behind the wheel, turns up AC/DC on the stereo, rolls the windows all the way down, and rips out of your driveway. When you haven't been able to get what you need through diplomatic means, your Fuck-it part will show up and take over like this. The problem is, Fuck-it causes the relational equivalent of speeding tickets, destructive collisions, and insurance premium hikes. It runs over innocent pedestrians and scares its passengers. It deserves some gratitude for being your ride or die and helping you find an alternative to defeat and neglect. But because it tends to take more extreme actions, it can harm your connection with the people you love and especially your connection with yourself. And there's always an Inner Critic hanging out in the back seat, ready to initiate a shame attack the minute your Fuck-it slows its roll.

Fears: If I don't grab what I want right now, I'll never get anything.

Hopes: My explosion of energy and determination will get me out of this stuck position, despite everything that tries to stop me.

Your Inner Mom can help notice your curiosity riding shotgun with your Fuck-it part, asking questions and maybe even helping it navigate a little. When your Fuck-it part begins to trust your curiosity, it will start sharing HOW MUCH PAIN you've been in and how far past your breaking point you really are. You'll help steer toward the compassion car wash, where some tears can flow, and a more honest conversation can happen. You will need to come up with a sustainable, realistic plan for addressing your unmet needs if you ever want to convince Fuck-it to hand over the keys. The two of you will take a deep, nourishing breath and offer your entire system some forgiveness for whatever mess may have been made, and then you'll call on your courage to begin to make repair.

GUILT

Guilt is a harsh poke from inside that tells you when you've stepped out of line with your own values or when you've inadvertently hurt someone who matters to you. It kicks in when you've transgressed or when you've centered your own desires and wanting ahead of others'. Prosocial, healthy guilt helps you notice areas where your actions or words may have violated your own integrity, and it offers you some internal motivation to make repair. It will prompt you to do the work of reconnecting and addressing mistakes. But if you, like so many of us, were conditioned to be a very good girl, then it's important to inquire with your Guilt part more deeply. Your Guilt can activate even when it's not warranted—when you have NOT actually transgressed or stepped out of line—just because you are violating social or familial expectations. Guilt wants you to come through in relationships—as a good mom, daughter, friend, partner, or employee—because it cares about preserving your integrity and your belonging.

Fears: If I don't meet others' expectations, I could lose them. Coming through for people who matter to me protects our connection.

Hopes: If I stay focused on meeting other people's needs, I won't lose their approval. I'll be safe in my belonging.

Your Inner Mom can help you recognize Guilt as a reminder of your drive to remain part of your pack—to not be rejected or abandoned, and to make sure you do right by others. When your Guilt part blooms inside you, you'll pause to consult your own integrity to determine if you're truly out of line—or just blazing new trails. Where you discover that your Guilt isn't warranted (because you haven't stepped out of integrity), you'll offer yourself compassion and encouragement to go ahead and explore. And when you have transgressed, you'll thank your Guilt part for letting you know, and you'll make relational repair with the person you've hurt.

INNER CRITIC

Your Inner Critic's job is to pick you apart and put you back together—better than ever. It has good intentions focused on self-improvement, but often gets its gears stuck and just loops on telling you what a POS you are. Your Inner Critic is a carbon copy of the people in your life who found fault with you when you were a child. It mimics the sentiments and tone of those harsh outer critics and repeats their message internally so that you will never forget exactly what kind of mistakes you could make. The Inner Critic's sole concern is ensuring you don't fail or embarrass yourself, and it's quick to tell you how you "should" be doing things. The Inner Critic doesn't trust that you have natural motivation for growth and development, and it's convinced that its harshness is necessary to keep you on a path to improvement. It sees a huge discrepancy between who you are and who you should be, and it can be especially brutal in its criticism of your mothering. Your IC will also find fault with your performance at work and as a spouse/partner, and certainly with your physical appearance. Despite its mean tone, what it wants more than anything is to make you pleasing to others and to help you hit all the important marks—so that you will never be rejected or abandoned.

Fears: If I stop noticing all my shortcomings and pushing to be better, I won't do well in life. I could easily slip into being not good enough.

Hopes: I'll fix all my flaws so that people will approve of me. I'll pick at my imperfections so that I can improve myself.

Your Inner Mom can help you listen to your Inner Critic with an open heart. You'll learn when it first experienced exclusion and loneliness, and as you soften toward it, your IC will start to trust you. You will become allies. You'll show it a new kind of strength and confidence that's rooted in unconditional love, helping it start to unpack its long history with shame and aloneness. Over time, your Inner Critic will move out of its dominant role and will become more of an editor in your life, a part that adds valuable awareness to how you show up in the world, chiming in with a much softer tone.

IRRITATED

An Irritated part is an alert to you that your boundaries were crossed. It's a mini alarm letting you know: This needs to stop. Your Irritated part registers the violation of those boundaries that have been trampled, ignored, and maybe even shat upon. It manifests viscerally in your body, letting you know THIS IS NOT OKAY, while still maintaining a semicomposed front. This part communicates its displeasure through your tone, word choice, movements, or volume, intending to make folks take notice before you have to open up a can of whoop ass. Your Irritated part doesn't like that you have to keep repeating yourself, repeating your work, and enduring unwanted stimulation.

Fears: I can't make it stop.

Hopes: Maybe by showing just a little anger, I can get this to stop.

Your Inner Mom can help you notice the edgy feeling in your body as an indication that a part of you can't take much more and needs to step away and get some relief. Your system is physically reaching overwhelm. You'll respect the alert, and even if you do reach a breaking point and lose your shit, you'll understand why, and you'll let your parts know that you get it. You're sorry for what they're going through. It IS too much. They do deserve some solitude and privacy. When your Irritated part is supported by your Inner Mom, it looks more like wisdom.

MAMA BEAR

Your Mama Bear shows up with physical and emotional power for her little ones to guard what needs protection, and she's not afraid to ROAR. Mama Bear takes her responsibility seriously and has a big presence. Sometimes her big presence can get ferociously protective when she senses a threat, and sometimes her big presence can be a furry refuge for little ones who need to feel safe. The early years of motherhood require a great deal of Mama Bear energy to keep helpless, dependent little ones alive and well. Mama Bear energy can take over the entirety of Mom's system and make it hard for her to shift into playful or relaxed states. She's devoted to her job, and she leads with her bravery and bigness, which distracts her attention away from how vulnerable she feels tending to her cubs.

Fears: If I don't roar and get big, my little one will be harmed.

Hopes: I'll be as big and bold as I need to be to keep everyone safe.

Your Inner Mom can help you remember that your Mama Bear's tender, vulnerable feelings exist underneath her roar, and you'll make sure to support her from inside, inquiring with her about how she feels threatened. You'll help her determine when she truly needs to roar, and you'll appreciate the hell out of her for it. And you'll pay attention to when she really just needs a hug.

MINIMIZER

Your Minimizer part is afraid of rejection and worried that you're "too much." It's an authenticity bypasser who shakes its head and denies that you're hurting, even while your wounds are throbbing with pain. It sweeps big emotions and internal reactions under the patriarchal rug and into isolation, where they remain, unacknowledged and uncared for. Driven by fear, your Minimizer attempts to hide your wounds because it doesn't believe it's safe to be anything but stoic or forgiving. It presents as tough and brave and can appear to be full of strength, but it causes you to betray your authenticity and tenderness. Your Minimizer is afraid of what would happen if you stopped and felt all the fear and hurt that are hanging out just in your periphery—and even more afraid of what would happen if you let others see your true distress. This part is not developed enough to know that as an adult, you have the capacity to be present with your pain without drowning in it—and that your compassionate presence is the thing that's so desperately needed.

Fears: If I show how much I hurt, I'll be seen as weak and unlikable.

Hopes: By downplaying my pain, I'll make myself more acceptable to others.

Your Inner Mom can help you start to notice ways your Minimizer has jumped in "to the rescue." When you recognize it—even several days after it's worked its magic—you'll start to see how it's so reflexive and conditioned that it just slipped itself in without you even noticing. You now have an opportunity to make amends with other parts of you who are hurting and feeling betrayed by your Minimizer. You will lift the rugs under which your vulnerability has been swept and coax out the banished, injured parts of you. You might come clean with people in your life about ways they have hurt you, or about new boundaries you're going to hold with them. You'll help your Minimizer know it's safer now to be honest about your true experiences. You'll inquire if your Minimizer might now prefer another line of work.

NUMBING

Your Numbing part helps you tune out when emotions feel overwhelming. It dulls your awareness so that you don't have to feel the discomfort, fear, or sadness that's swirling inside you. It's the one who prompts you to pour a glass of wine, pick up your phone and start scrolling, reach for the bag of chips, or turn on Netflix—to create a buffer when it senses you need a break from difficult feelings. Your Numbing part kicks in when life feels too intense or when you're emotionally overloaded—it activates whenever it determines you need a psychological time-out. This part senses overwhelm in ways that may, upon deeper examination, surprise you. It is often quite young, reflexively believing that you need protection from difficult emotion or sensation. It brings a sense of spacing out or mental fog, which makes it challenging to get to know, since it can cloud your consciousness with distraction or haziness that's not particularly conducive to connection.

Fears: I don't have the capacity to feel this pain or unsettledness; it's too much.

Hopes: If I disconnect from my awareness, I won't have to feel this feeling.

Your Inner Mom can help you bring the brightness of new curiosity to your spacey moments, to your disconnected or disembodied experiences, lighting those areas up with more consciousness. You will slowly start to illuminate the nebulous territory where your Numbing part tried to blur the contours of what happened to you. You'll begin to revere these strange areas as sacred spots where your Numbing part pulled you to safety, and you'll come back in a pilgrimage to these mysterious sites. You'll begin to make out more details of light against dark as you observe the dust settling and new forms taking shape. You'll breathe clean oxygen into the space, updating your fearful part: *I'm here now.*

PANIC

Panic is afraid of your fear. This part pulls the alarm when it senses emergency. It wants to get you the fuck out of the scary feeling you find yourself in, and it commandeers your physiology in any and every way it needs to in order to distance you from the threat STAT. As the alarm starts to sound, Panic feels even more alarmed (!) and it accelerates your heartbeat and hijacks your breathing, turning your body into a strange animal that frightens itself. This highly charged, primal protector has tons of physical vitality that takes over your eyes, ears, voice, and viscera, readying you for flight, freeze, or fawn. The end result of all this intense activation is that Panic becomes a lonely, relationally disconnected part that operates in isolation. It needs and wants more than anything to be brought back to slowness and safety.

Fears: If I don't get out of this situation, I might die.

Hopes: If I escalate and amplify my internal chemistry, I might be able to save myself.

Your Inner Mom can help when you feel Panic take over your physiology, by offering a validating safety check. With her steadiness, your Inner Mom will assess whether you're truly in danger, and if you are, she'll support you in using all the lifesaving chemistry that Panic provides to propel you to safety. When the emergency has passed, or if it was a false alarm, your Inner Mom will give your Panic part some gratitude for being a brave first responder and then shift into updating it and helping it relax. Let Panic know you recognize its commitment to saving your life. Show it that you survived, you're safe now, and it's not alone.

PERFECTIONIST

The Perfectionist is in cahoots with your Inner Critic and takes the IC's improvement plan to the next level, pushing you to get everything exactly right. Your Perfectionist uses stress hormones and negative self-talk to motivate you, which means you have to disconnect from your tenderness and ignore some of your real needs. This keenly observant part was witness to your childhood struggle and never wants you to feel that kind of suffering again. It holds you to the highest standards now, to avoid failure, rejection, and humiliation. Always comparing you to everyone else, this part creates an undertone of competitive energy in your relationships. The Perfectionist doesn't believe it's safe to have flaws or to just be "good enough." It will continue to believe that your belonging on earth is contingent on your stellar performance—which your kids will internalize as their own north star too. When you find the courage to introduce your Perfectionist to the grief and shame you've been dodging, your humanness will finally have some space to emerge.

Fears: If I'm not perfect, I will lose everything that matters.

Hopes: By being exceptional and excelling at everything, I will be valued and feel loved.

Your Inner Mom can help you offer your Perfectionist the respect and admiration it deserves. To win its trust, you will have to demonstrate your ability to stay warm and kind when you encounter your feelings of failure and shame. As your capacity for acceptance grows, your Perfectionist will start to sense more safety in slowing down, admitting defeat, and asking for help. You will invite it to lie down in the warm grass under the blue sky for longer and longer stretches of time, where it will have a chance to observe the world around it and start to explore the unconditional love that it never knew existed.

RAGE

When your protectors have done EVERYTHING they can to manage circumstances and none of it worked, Rage shows up to get back some fucking control. As a mom, you spend so much energy giving and sacrificing, and Rage knows you do indeed have limits, boundaries, and needs—and those limits, boundaries, and needs have been neglected or disrespected for too long. Rage experiences this violation of you as having crossed the line from tolerable frustration or irritation into emergency territory. It's like a firefighter called to an event where its job is to PUT OUT THE FIRE—even if doors need to be smashed down and vintage heirlooms and antique treasures have to be destroyed in the process. It lacks finesse, but it's absolutely determined to be effective—and it escalates to this extreme expression because it doesn't believe there's a choice. As a younger, less-developed part of you, it's possible that Rage may be mistaking this current situation for something awful that happened in your past, when you were small and powerless. What it truly wants is relief and change.

Fears: If I don't erupt, I will just continue to be used, disrespected, and unappreciated.

Hopes: By unleashing unequivocally, I will regain some power.

Your Inner Mom can help you remember that Rage appears when it senses your legitimate boundaries, limits, and needs are being violated. Now you can honor its efforts to get you back to safety and wholeness. You'll recognize that Rage is a young part that believes you have no power—and you'll show it how you can now speak on its behalf so that it isn't forced to speak for you. Rage doesn't know it has the adult YOU as an advocate who can care about it, even if the rest of the world doesn't understand or support you. Good questions for Rage: *What boundaries have been crossed that need to be respected? What are you afraid would happen to me if you didn't get enraged? How can I help hold those boundaries?* Rage is here to give you the energy to fight for yourself: Rage may be acting out to get others' attention, but it's YOUR attention it needs most of all.

REGRET

Regret is sadness or grief managed and manhandled by your Inner Critic. Regret has one foot in courage, which allows you to acknowledge honestly how much you're hurting. But it has the other foot firmly planted in self-blame, which keeps it looping on a story about your poor judgment or wrongdoing. Regret believes it can help you feel better by locating the error you made and rubbing your nose in it one more time. Control is the drug of choice for Regret, and it's hooked on the fantasy that there's something you could've, would've, or should've done differently to avoid the vulnerability you're feeling now. When Regret gets extreme, it can take on Destroyer/Fuck-it vibes and try to entirely remove your vulnerability, hoping to eliminate exposure, loss, and humiliation for the rest of time.

Fears: If I don't focus on the mistake that was made and the part I played in all of it, I'll just keep hurting like this.

Hopes: By focusing on this mistake and my own responsibility in making it, I imagine that I can change it somehow.

Your Inner Mom can help you recognize Regret as an aversion to shame and grief. When it's jonesing for control, you'll bring it more courage to be with the grief and the shame that are waiting for your warmth. And when it trusts the softness of your compassion, Regret will untangle into separate strands of loss and longing, both of which can find a home in your tender heart.

RESENTFUL

A Resentful part is full of unacknowledged fury. It's held back in a choke hold by other parts, like your Minimizer, Superwoman, Perfectionist, and Controller, who are trying to make sure you're a GOOD mom. Resentment festers like an infection; it doesn't have permission to be seen or expressed, and so it lurks beneath the surface, growing in substance and severity. Resentful juices cause a general acidity in your system and bring sourness to your primary relationships. When the social rules about motherhood do not allow for honesty, your truths get swallowed down but never forgotten. This part navigates the very thin line between being honest (*I'm pissed off!*) and staying safe (*Keep a lid on it*). Your Resentful part is a Fuck-it part in the making. It hangs on to the tiny thread of power it believes you have: the power to hold a grudge. Though it's unpopular for bringing so much sourness to you and your relationships, your Resentful part is committed to you and deserves a medal for how it never abandons your truth, even when it knows it's not safe to express it.

Fears: It's dangerous to be angry, and I don't have the power to change what's not working for me.

Hopes: By keeping the fire of my fury stoked, I will not lose hope—and maybe other people will finally pay attention to what I need.

Your Inner Mom can help you extend appreciation to your Resentful part for not letting the flame of your fury die, even when it hasn't been safe to be furious. In the presence of your courage and confidence, your Resentful part will recognize that its grudges can be released into the truths that it has been longing to express. Telling the truth releases Resentment from its choke hold and gives you access to greater calm and connectedness.

RESPONSIBLE

Your Responsible part is a brave, self-sacrificing inner child who wants more than anything to be able to save the day but is not truly empowered. In fact, a Responsible part is often a parentified inner child who is too young, undeveloped, and small to hold the weight of the role. As a result, it is set up to fail. While it projects competence, your Responsible part secretly lacks confidence; it feels burdened and concerned about its ability to shoulder the job it's been assigned. Your Responsible part is very serious and quick to sing a song of self-blame when things don't go well, joining voices with a shaming Inner Critic who is happy to lend its pipes for the chorus. Lurking beneath a presentation of willingness and humility, your young Responsible part harbors a quiet worry that it doesn't have what it takes.

Fears: Things will fall apart if I don't shoulder this burden.

Hopes: If I can handle this job effectively, things won't fall apart. I'll be safe and maybe loved (or at least not hated).

Your Inner Mom can help you befriend your Responsible part and let it know how much you appreciate its willingness to show up and work hard. You can introduce this part to your adult empowerment and present-day resources. You can share your warmth with it and let it know you can be with whatever comes—even shame and grief. It no longer has to sacrifice itself to save you. You are here to hold the reins.

SAD

Sad is a simple but soulful part that doesn't come with a lot of complications. It's small and vulnerable, and it needs to be scooped up, understood, and offered comfort. Sadness is unavoidable in life and does not require fixing. It's very human. That said, when your Sad part is left alone, with no company and no soft place to land, its despair can become huge and all-consuming. Your Sad part needs your presence and warmth so it can share the truth it knows about the contours of your tender, hurting heart. It's privy to your Wanting and can contribute greatly to clarifying what's most important to you in life. Listen closely.

Fears: My hurting could completely take me over.

Hopes: If the soulfulness in my sadness can be embraced, I'll feel whole again.

Your Inner Mom can help you meet your Sad part with an open heart when it shows up. You'll slow things down and make a soft space beside you to offer this Inner Baby part some comfort and safety to feel how it feels. You'll resist the urge to cheer it up or fix it, instead giving it the gift of simply being present with it. You will remember that sadness points directly to what you value most, and you'll recognize it as a friend who knows you well. When your Sad part is supported by your Inner Mom, it tells you the truth and brings humility and soulfulness to your life.

SCARED

Your Scared part needs you to listen to it. It shows up with an adrenaline-infused announcement, intended as an urgent request for you to slow down and pay attention to what it's feeling afraid of and what it's bracing for. Scared is a young Inner Baby part, and it doesn't feel equipped to enter into the threatening territory ahead, all alone. It needs the company of someone stronger and braver who has its back. It's often feeling spooked about things that happened in the past, in which case we can hear it out and help update it, clearing the past out of the present. But sometimes it fears physical or emotional pain tied to an upcoming event. A scared part does not need convincing, controlling, or fixing. It needs company and care, steadiness and presence. There is a truth that it needs to communicate, and it requires our respect and attention. Being Scared isn't inherently traumatizing; being left all alone with terror is.

Fears: I'm not safe. I need help and I don't want to be all alone.

Hopes: By sharing my fear, I can get help and companionship. I won't be alone.

Your Inner Mom can help you approach your Scared part with reverence and respect. You'll find out if there's anything specific it needs from you and offer your care and presence so that it is not alone. When your Scared part is supported by your Inner Mom, it gratefully tells you the story it's been believing. Embracing your Scared part expands your empathy and compassion, which your kids will directly benefit from. Your Scared part is sacred parts in disguise.

SELF-DOUBT

Self-doubt is here to help you belong. It shows up when you feel wobbly and offers you steadiness by telling you that there is a RIGHT way to do things—you just have to find a trustworthy *external* voice to follow. Self-doubt doesn't know that YOU are trustworthy. If you didn't feel known and understood growing up, you had to develop a Self-doubting part to help you survive emotionally. It developed a strategy: Defer to others, and abandon trust in your own perspective. Self-doubt's specialty is discarding your gut instincts so you can stay in connection with people who don't understand you. When you were young, you had no better choice. Self-doubt chose connection over authenticity—and got neither. Now you can offer *internal* steadiness to all your parts and find the folks who really get you.

Fears: If I don't doubt myself, I'll feel disconnected from the people around me. I'll be left alone.

Hopes: By questioning myself, I leave room for others to be right and stay good. This feels hopeful because I believe my life depends on those shaky connections.

Your Inner Mom can help you recognize that Self-doubt shows up when you're looking outside for secure connection and not finding it. You'll see Self-doubt as a reminder that your Inner Mom can now be your secure attachment figure, and you can offer your Inner Baby parts all the attention and resonance they've been missing. Understanding Self-doubt as a cry for connection will allow you to stop trying to get your Inner Baby's needs met by unqualified people. You can start respecting your intuition, and you can believe yourself.

SUICIDAL

Your Suicidal part is trying to save you. It exists to offer you an escape from despair by helping you to end this pain. When absolutely no other way appears to be open to you, your Suicidal part will turn complete powerlessness and unbearable suffering into what feels like the only empowered move it can make—which is a drastic and devastating one. Your Suicidal part believes there is no good way out of the pain you're in—but it also cares about you enough to get you out of this suffering. Ask your Suicidal part if it would be open to other forms of support, and let it know that plenty of moms who have a Suicidal part have discovered ways to feel better. There is someone out there who can help you so that this part doesn't have to feel like it's your only option. One of the most powerful things about IFS is the normalization and welcoming of *all* parts, even Suicidal ones. That said, we want to encourage you to seek immediate care if you are feeling suicidal. You deserve to live with more ease. Call a trusted friend or call 911 or the 988 Lifeline.

Fears: The pain I'm feeling and causing is intolerable.

Hopes: My suffering will end. My family won't be burdened by me anymore and might miss me or more fully understand my pain.

Your Inner Mom can help bring tenderness to your Suicidal part, who you realize now has been trying to save you in its own way. You'll thank your Suicidal part for giving you a sense of choice and a way out of your pain. You'll no longer see it as pathological but instead as a friend who shows up to try to help you when it believes you're in a hopeless bind. You'll let it feel your warmth and allyship, and you'll look for someone trustworthy and nonjudgmental to help you hold your pain so that you and your Suicidal part can be understood, respected, and cared for. You are not alone.

SUPERWOMAN

Your Superwoman part is truly magnificent. Her magnificence is both grand and grandiose, leading her to deny any weakness or fragility. She is committed to being highly proactive in guarding your soft, tender center, projecting a larger-than-life aura of type A competence and self-reliance. Through disappointing and painful experiences with others, this part has learned that it's not safe to be vulnerable or to count on people to come through for you. While she feels deeply injured, she doesn't let anyone see how she's hurting. Superwoman has a mandate to always take care of business, be on top of things, complete projects (regardless of the cost to you), rise to all occasions, not accept "handouts," and never show weakness. She bears the weight of the world but doesn't show off her muscles—or her weight-bearing injuries. Superwoman craves rescue and recognition but hides her craving masterfully, which can make her appear defensive and intimidating to others. She has access to lots of creativity, courage, and confidence to fuel and sustain her but she's a lonely leader. She simmers in low-grade resentment toward everyone who disappoints her, unaware of how she blocks connection.

Fears: I'm completely alone in this.

Hopes: By doing everything and doing it well, I won't have to notice how alone I feel.

Your Inner Mom can help you earn the trust of this hardworking part who has had to do EVERYTHING on her own up until this point. Your ability to see her and validate her will be a soothing balm for her weary muscles. Superwoman hasn't felt recognized or supported enough, and your witnessing of her magnificence will allow her to gradually venture into vulnerability, where her grief and shame are hanging out. (She will need your compassion and tenderness with those.) When it's safe for her to relax her grip, she will discover there's more space for connection to grow in her relationships.

WANTING

Wanting reminds you what you're longing for. Your Wanting part came with you into this life and is closely connected with psychological and emotional hunger for intimacy and connection, for being deeply seen and known, for being satisfied and fulfilled. It's primally alive with your animal needs and tinged with desire for pleasure. When Wanting gets pushed away, it aches with envy, scarcity, and shame about its desires—and your Angry part shows up, furious about all the unmet needs. Wanting can be present-day, and it can also be from the past, existing inside of your Inner Baby, reminding you of your emotional hunger. When Wanting attaches itself to other people, outcomes, experiences, substances, or objects, it outsources your power. When it's respected, it will infuse your life with sparkle and authentic, connected energy.

Fears: This void cannot be filled. I'm longing for something that I may not be able to get.

Hopes: I know what I need, and I can get it.

Your Inner Mom can help you have the courage to inquire into what your Wanting part is truly longing for. You'll learn what it's missing from your early childhood in the form of connection, intimacy, and belonging. These childhood needs can't be met by others now that you're an adult—but they can be met through your own attuned and loving attention. You'll become devoted to your Wanting, helping it be seen, known, and tended to in the present day. When your Wanting part gets supported by your Inner Mom, it breathes new life into your world.

Chapter 6

The Good Mom/Bad Mom Loop

Before you were a mom, you only had to worry about yourself. You were the head coach of one team—your own. Team ME! When you became a mom, all of a sudden you found yourself managing multiple lives and using your singular nervous system to regulate all kinds of additional needs, wants, and distress signals coming in from every angle, around the clock. Your system of parts had to adapt—dramatically.

Responsibility is usually the first protector—a sort of team captain— to find itself elevated into a leadership position in a new mom's system. It anxiously takes on what feels like a massive burden. Good moms aren't supposed to call their kids burdens, but the Responsible part is, by definition, totally responsible and pretty freaking burdened! They're driven to not screw up, and they take that job verrrry seriously. The baby's precarious vulnerability lands like a slippery load (danger) in Responsibility's shaky little arms, and news starts to spread outward to the entire system: "Um, can I have your attention, please? This is very vulnerable! And dangerous!" Your whole neighborhood of parts begins to buzz and hum with the electricity of danger. All your parts who are inclined toward caregiving and control are notified, and they start to gather in ways they believe will be helpful for the cause.

Yes, you may be outwardly cooing and reveling in your new baby, but somewhere close by, your Responsible part is monitoring and managing much baby-related data and the high level of stress that goes with its position as senior manager of danger. It's considering how the baby can't hold up its head, throws up half of what it eats, breathes erratically through the night, and cries even when you've bounced it in your arms for two hours straight. Your Inner Critic, Self-doubt, and Anxious parts will start assembling to take on the task of reminding you of their CONCERNS frequently and loudly: Your primary job in life is to ensure the safety and wellness of your child, and that child is helpless, wholly dependent on you (of all people!), and you could fuck this up at any moment.

Together, these parts form a new team—Team Kid—the foundation of your good-mom identity. Team Kid immediately drops the quotation marks from "good mom" and "bad mom" and sets up black-and-white thinking as its primary operating system. As a mom, either you're Good or you're Bad. Period.

Team Kid has a deep bench of manager parts who are masters at selflessness. They're here to make sure that you're doing all the right mom-related stuff. These are the parts that start telling you that you need to seriously up your game, or you will risk being a bad mom. Team Kid parts are wildly child-centered (remember—your parts don't care how old your kid is; you can have a thirty-seven-year-old child, and from the perspective of these Good Mom parts, that kid is still your baby). This can-do team attracts parts who share a primary interest: Keep your kid at the forefront of everything and ensure that your child is safe and well. Team Kid is definitely right about one thing: When your child is little, they are HIGHLY vulnerable, and they do need constant care. Team Kid parts hijack your attention, bring on the anxiety and guilt, and drive you into caretaking mode. Dominant and vigilant, they scan for danger and keep their figurative eyes on your child pretty much all the time.

When they're most relaxed, they're highly interested in your kid; when they're super activated, they're panicky about your kid—or panicky about how you're failing your kid. But on some level, all the Team Kid protectors are focused on improving your performance, and they vibrate with a certain amount of fear and inner criticism. It feels unfair that when you become a parent, you sign up for a life of terror and negative self-talk, but it's true. We go into this motherhood thing thinking that babies bring nuzzling and sweetness, and kids bring connection and fun. And they do. But they also bring terror and insecurity. Or at least a high degree of unsettled preoccupation. That preoccupying fear comes from two places: your awareness of your present-day child's real-time vulnerability and your own personal history with vulnerability (Inner Baby stuff from your past).

As you learned in chapter 3, when you become a mom, your Inner Baby comes knocking at your door, ringing the bell repeatedly until you answer. And even if you don't open the door willingly, the door will ultimately be blasted off its hinges. Your Inner Baby will drag its funky old psychology over the threshold and into the sanctity of your living room, where it will proceed to unpack all your unfinished business from the past. Suddenly, your old shit is everywhere, strewn about hither and yon, and you can barely find a clean spot on the sofa to sit down and collect your thoughts. Team Kid parts are witness to this messy, emotional baggage of yours that has now reappeared out of the blue. Your Inner Baby is crying for comfort and is protesting current conditions—and your real-life 3D baby is usually crying too. All that noise is precisely what Team Kid is here to quiet. Your Good Mom parts snap to attention and start doing their thing. Anxious, Caretaker, Perfectionist, and Fixer parts take charge to help you get the job done and clean up your vulnerable mess.

What Drives the Good Mom Machine?

Moms have plenty of physiology driving their protective impulses, which are designed to keep their brains attuned to the health and well-being of their children. These internal teams don't operate in a vacuum—they're responding to a culture that simultaneously demands intensive mothering while providing minimal support. The "good mom" standard has never been higher, while the village that once raised children has largely disappeared. This cultural pressure amplifies your Team Kid parts, who want you to do everything right, all the time, in service of your vulnerable child—and in service of your desire to be a good mom (the world is watching; you don't want to be like your own mom; you could totally fuck this up). They inhibit certain of your natural impulses and desires, and they talk harshly and critically inside your head to try to keep you in line. Team Kid parts can make you feel like you're doing a great job by working so hard and sacrificing so much (go, selfless parts!), or they can make you feel like you are failing miserably as they compare you to all the other moms (boo, selfish parts!). Your Anxious part and your Inner Critic rule the streets in Team Kid–ville, and those Good Mom parts lead to exhaustion, imbalance, and burnout, which propel you directly into your breaking point.

> ✳ The parts of you who work so hard to make you a good mom are the ones that are the meanest to you. Good Mom parts can tip you out of balance and into burnout.

All moms know from lived experience that being led by Team Kid means that your own needs are pushed aside. Peeing when you've got to go? Hold it a little longer. Crying when you need to cry? Not now. Yelling when you're angry? Not if you're a good mom. Going on vacation without your kids? Um, really? Your growling stomach, aches and pains, exhaustion, and personal desires become background noise as these parts laser focus you on your child's needs—again and again. They aim to keep your baby or child thriving, but they might also turn you into a depleted shell of yourself in the process. Knowing and understanding why they're here, how they're trying to help, and also how they can easily become unbalanced and hyperfunctional will give you more empowerment and choice within your inner world. When Team Kid operates from a balanced place, these parts help you attune beautifully to your child's needs, respond with patience during difficult moments, and create the consistency children thrive on. The problem isn't that these parts exist—it's that they often work without breaks, boundaries, or backup.

The Uprising: Team *What About Mom?!*

But here's what every mother discovers: You can only suppress your own needs for so long before something inside you snaps back. At some point, you get fed up with all the withholding and all the internal trash-talking being perpetrated by your Team Kid parts, who wish your Wanting would die so you could stay focused on Fixing and Caretaking and just be a good mom allllll the time. And that's when a whole different group of parts with an entirely opposite agenda starts to organize a little infrastructure of its own, running some imaginary plays in your mind and gathering steam in the form of resentment. These parts want you to get a hit of dopamine and satisfaction or a burst of power and recognition or maybe just a fucking break—some rest, relief, or recreation. Things have gotten unbalanced and caustic in your Team Kid–driven inner world, and these parts—Team *What About Mom?!*— are all about soothing and relieving you. They're known around town as selfish parts. They remember that you used to be on your own team, and they've noticed that you don't show up for practice anymore. These parts take matters into their own hands, flipping on the lights in the empty stadium of the silent and deserted venue once referred to as YOU. "*What about Mom?!*" they scream into the void.

Team *What About Mom?!* parts remember that you had a life and likely a more gratifying one—before you were a mom. They haven't forgotten the blissful feelings of power, freedom, and gratification, and they aren't afraid to move in and reclaim a little of your autonomy. Team *What About Mom?!* sees how your power, ease, and privacy are going down the tubes due to your overdetermined efforts to be a good mom. They witness how precarious your good-mom position is; they see that you can't possibly sustain this level of selflessness. When you absolutely can no longer continue self-sacrificing, these are the parts that burst forth. They don't feel like they have a choice. They cut you loose so that you can draw some unmistakably clear lines, or even yell and scream, completely shut down, slam the door, drink a third glass of wine, or disappear from the scene. After two hours of patiently mediating sibling fights, something snaps and they take over: *I don't give a damn who started it. Both of you go to your rooms right now! I'm done with this bullshit!*

They want what they want when they want it, and they only care about you—which is manna for a system that's been so starved. These are the parts Team Kid despises and shames—your "Bad Mom" parts, the ones that are so legitimately BAD in the eyes of your Inner Critic that they've fallen completely out of those quotation marks. Your Inner Critic will tell you—there's nothing debatable about their badness.

While Team *What About Mom?!* parts *can* be destructive, they're also the ones who help you set necessary boundaries, advocate for your needs, and prevent complete self-annihilation. Sometimes what looks like "selfish" behavior is actually healthy self-preservation.

The relationship between these teams moves beyond conflict into polarization—a state where each side becomes so threatened by the other that coexistence feels impossible. Team Kid operates as if any trace of selfishness will contaminate your goodness, while Team *What About Mom?!* experiences your self-sacrificial impulses as a direct threat to your freedom, power, or maybe even survival.

For clarification, Team *What About Mom?!* is not the same as "Team Self-Care." These parts aren't restful or subtle; they don't show up to encourage a warm bath or a few deep breaths. No. They're impulsive and compulsive and willing to go big. Team *What About Mom?!* parts are disinhibitors. They have an agenda to release all the pressure that your Team Kid parts have been creating inside your system. All that self-sacrifice and caregiving be damned. Get outta the way: Team *What About Mom?!* is on the scene, taking the lids off the boiling pots and throwing out the baby with the bathwater. Here's how your internal dialogue might sound at your breaking point when your inner teams go to war:

> **Team Kid:** You should be grateful for these precious moments. Other moms would give anything for this time.
>
> **Team *What About Mom?!*:** I haven't had five minutes to myself in weeks. I'm desperate just to pee by myself.
>
> **Team Kid:** Selfish. This is what you signed up for when you became a mom.
>
> **Team *What About Mom?!*:** I signed up to be a mom, not to have my body and emotions constantly invaded!

As you may know from experience, disinhibited, reactive mom behavior doesn't go over well—inside of you or outside of you. Your Bad Mom parts immediately start hearing from Team Kid—who continues to tear you a new one for stepping out of line. And as your Team *What About Mom?!* parts remain on the receiving end of viciously negative self-talk, they understandably get tired of hearing it. These parts know about all the resources, attention, and time that your child (and everyone else) is receiving, and they're very aware that you're getting the short end of the stick. They remember that you are a person who has needs that have nothing to do with your child. They're scared and mad about all you've lost and all you continue to lose, and they're determined to get you some dopamine or a sedative, or whatever it is that will put you out of your good-mom misery.

Team *What About Mom?!* parts are occasionally subtle, but they can also get extreme and make you look and feel out of control. They're the ones you make efforts to hide. When you unblend from them, you can see their good intentions and how they're trying to rescue you. They know there's something you need that you're not getting, and they're worried about you. They watch you bending over backward and still feeling guilty and unappreciated. They're acutely aware of your unmet needs—and they decide it's time to do something about it.

Riding the Roller Coaster

When your parts work really hard to make you good, there will be an equal and opposite reaction to let off the pressure. "Bad" parts take over and do damage. Next comes the cleanup crew—the hardworking Good Mom parts—who try to fix the damage that was done. This creates an internal pendulum swing between extremes, with an invisible scorekeeper inside tracking every maternal misstep and demanding correction.

Team Kid parts are omnipresent, making sure you keep delivering as a good mom. And then your freaking Inner Baby shows up with its messy baggage strewn all over your baby's nursery, pulling you into an emotional time warp and making you wildly unsettled. All the while, you have to keep mothering. Your child is hungry or unhappy or injured, and the world's eyes are on you. There's pressure to perform and to be selfless. Your Team Kid parts start using some serious muscle to inhibit or disown any semblance of selfishness unbefitting motherhood. Here's where parts like the Controller, Minimizer, Caretaker, and Guilt become a good mom's best friends. These Team Kid parts take over the task of exiling your Inner Baby parts and keeping you focused on self-sacrificing, good-mom behaviors.

Components of the Loop

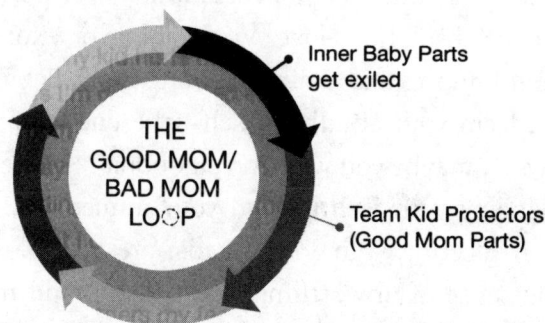

THE
GOOD MOM/
BAD MOM
LOOP

Inner Baby Parts
get exiled

Team Kid Protectors
(Good Mom Parts)

As your Team Kid parts lead you straight into the barren land of self-sacrifice, they do so with a weighty agenda. Team Kid and its self-sacrificing ways may appear on the surface to be all about your child—all about dialing in what's maternally best, attuning to your kid's needs, and supporting their optimal growth and development. Mom's child-centered efforts most certainly do include altruism and benevolence. But there's more to it. Team Kid parts are still, in fact, YOUR parts, designed by YOUR system, to help YOU make it in this world. Every single protector part has an agenda—it's there to try to change, affect, prevent, and shape events, according to your best interests. Protectors are here to *do* stuff. They aren't like Inner Baby parts, who exist largely in feelings, and they aren't like your Inner Mom, who can just hold space for what's here and stay present and feel compassion. No. Protectors all have an angle.

Team Kid operates with an unconscious "give to get" formula: *If I sacrifice enough, I'll finally be seen as valuable. If I'm patient enough, I'll prove my worth. If I give until it hurts, maybe I'll finally be recognized as a good mom.* When we bring curiosity to our Team Kid protectors and we inquire about their hopes, fears, and beliefs, we discover that our protectors' actions are motivated by very personal experiences that predate motherhood and have roots in our individual histories of love and loss. Our selfless parts have their hearts set on getting something meaningful out of all this giving.

Buried inside all the good-mom behavior is your Inner Baby, secretly attending to your wish for redemption—or possibly forgiveness, fulfillment, absolution, love, vindication, or exoneration—for yourself. The inhibiting and exiling of your Inner Baby can be part of a plot to redeem your childhood self—the one who was told she was too needy. Or maybe you were too emotional? Self-centered? Dramatic? By silencing your feelings and your unmet needs and focusing instead on meeting your kid's needs, are you hoping to erase an underlying sense of unworthiness or badness and maybe finally gain their approval (whoever *they* are)? If the goal is to be valued in another's eyes, and your pesky Inner Baby is getting in the way of you showing up and delivering, then you better shut that BS down.

Only you can't. Nevertheless, she—your Inner Baby—persists. And your Good Mom parts get louder and meaner in an effort to shut her up, creating a hostile environment inside your own psychology. Team Kid becomes self-contemptuous, and your Inner Baby absorbs the hate and the abuse. The more Team Kid ramps up its efforts to control and improve things, the worse your Inner Baby feels and the more desperate things become.

When You Literally Can't Anymore

When too many demands from inside and outside compete for your energy and attention all at once, moms use the word "overwhelm" to describe their experience. Overwhelm is a kind of forced surrender when you feel robbed of capacity and yet continually hammered by more requests, requirements, commands, and stimulation. Overwhelm feels like failure. It's that place in your physiological psychology where you feel forced to split. Something has to be sacrificed. Here, at your breaking point, something that's precious to you gets compromised. That compromise is a loss. It's sad. But moms tend to interpret that kind of loss not as sadness, but as failure.

Your values, your physical needs, your goodness, your dignity, your tenderness, your focus—something has to give. So your parts divide into teams and polarize against each other. Something tender is exiled so that you don't lose or screw up something else that's also precious and tender. You allocate your attention to one thing at the expense of another. It's you or your child. Who's gonna take one for the team? Which team's gonna win? Your nervous system decides for you, and it isn't consensual.

The internal war around the allocation of your dwindling resources is the fertile soil in which so much guilt, shame, resentment, and distress take root. It's hard to reach your breaking point and not feel like you've failed.

FYI, it's not possible to avoid this territory. At some point, you just will max out and your parts will polarize and you will make mistakes—maybe big ones. You will miss important moments and critical cues with your child. You'll run out of energy and ideas and desire at times. You might yell or scream. There will be things you regret. This moment of crisis, though painful, is actually where transformation becomes possible.

✳ You have a nervous system, which means you have a breaking point. You can't wish that away or argue with the fact that you have real limits.

Almost all the moms we see in our practices report feeling overwhelmed on the regular, sometimes even as a baseline. They bring themselves into therapy because they've reached a breaking point and are beyond their limit and past their capacity to metabolize their inner experience, and they feel like they're failing. Moms report that their breaking point feels like a physical switch in their system, where Good Mom parts abruptly hand over the keys to Bad Mom parts.

Components of the Loop

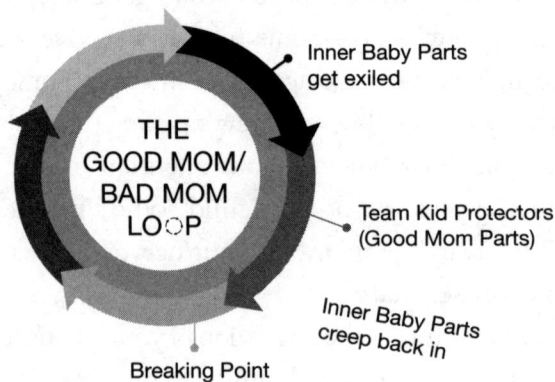

THE GOOD MOM/ BAD MOM LOOP

Inner Baby Parts get exiled

Team Kid Protectors (Good Mom Parts)

Inner Baby Parts creep back in

Breaking Point

At her breaking point, Mom has reached some level of crisis. She's been juggling everything she thinks she needs to do to qualify as a good mom, along with all the wanting, fear, and sadness of her own tumultuous life, and guess what: It's too much to hold at once. Some balls are about to get dropped. The question is, Which ones? Team Kid is intent on making sure you do NOT drop any balls related to good mothering. Mom's Inner Critic starts making announcements on her loudspeaker:

DON'T YOU DARE SNAP RIGHT NOW! HOLD YOUR SHIT TOGETHER OR ELSE YOU'RE GOING TO SCREW UP YOUR KIDS AND IT WILL BE ALL YOUR FAULT!

Inside, her Inner Baby parts are trembling or crying, remembering how it felt when she was small, helpless, and alone. They're infusing her with all kinds of intense emotion that's begging her to slow down and get soft. But it's hard to slow down and get soft when you're also exiting the grocery store, trying to wrangle a toddler who's tantrumming and another kid who's moaning about needing a third cookie while someone's waiting for your parking spot, honking impatiently, and you haven't unloaded the groceries from the cart yet. And you skipped lunch. That's just not fun. Not really doable. Right?

In predicaments like these where there are many loud, needy voices ricocheting around in their inner and outer worlds, moms come face-to-face with their old patterns of coping and reacting left over from childhood. Scream? Collapse? Strike out? Run away? How did your system learn to react when you were little and you felt cornered and powerless and alone? That shit's gonna reappear again and again. Which sucks. It's so hard to continually reencounter your breaking point and your primitive reactions—only now, you feel like how you handle these difficult moments matters so much more. Your kids are watching. They're on the receiving end of whatever your parts do (PRESSURE). They're even more vulnerable than you (DANGER). You don't want to be like your parents and just keep handing down the same injuries to your kids (DANGER and PRESSURE).

Are your Good Mom parts going to be able to hold steady in the face of hearing Junior yell over and over, "I want another cookie.

You're a mean mommy!" while the lookie-loos push their tidy carts slowly past you and the guy waiting for your spot starts honking, trying to spur your shit show into faster action? Probably not. You probably can't be a Caretaker or a Perfectionist in that moment. You also probably can't collapse into an Inner Baby meltdown and just hit the ground sobbing. Not really an option. We're going to guess that it's your Team *What About Mom?!* parts that will burst onto the scene right about now, here to salvage some of your power and get you out of the hideous, desperate vulnerability and humiliation you're feeling.

Which Bad Mom part shows up? It could very well be Rage, who grabs your toddler and starts wrestling them into their car seat. A Blamer would do nicely now too, with some choice words for your cookie monster to help off-load some of this embarrassment you're feeling. Fuck-it is ready to take that grocery cart full of kale and cookies and shove it fast and hard between all the Teslas and just drive (the fuck) away. This is your breaking point.

At your breaking point—in a crisis of overwhelm—your nervous system is forced to make some budget cuts. Some Good Mom parts get laid off immediately with no notice and no severance pay. Your singular nervous system, magnificent as it is, cannot physically meet the needs and requirements of these multiple competing demands. It's not possible. You heard it here. It's not possible.

Your breaking point defines and describes a polarization between your Good Mom and Bad Mom parts. You will feel magnetically pulled by one team or the other. More likely than not, you'll get swept up by your Bad Mom parts, and you'll find yourself getting reactive in ways your Good Mom parts aren't proud of. Your Inner Baby parts will be split off and abandoned. This will look and feel very much like all the worst things that happened to you when you were small, and it will give you a lingering, crummy feeling of being complicit in that legacy of pain that just keeps getting handed down in your family line.

When you're exhausted, regressed, scared, or depleted, you inch closer to your breaking point, where the energetic baton gets handed off from Team Kid to Team *What About Mom?!* All the maternal managing, performing, producing, fixing, maintaining, and helping depletes the system and brings Mom's Good Mom machinery to a grinding halt. There is no more to give. Out of gas. Just fucking done.

✳ Your breaking point defines and describes a polarization between your Good Mom and Bad Mom parts.

The Takeover

Your breaking point happens at the juncture of physical depletion and ongoing stressful circumstances. That could mean your complete exhaustion encountering a crying, complaining child. That could mean your calorically low reality colliding with your child's caffeinated intensity. It could mean the excruciating pain of stepping on yet another LEGO with a bare foot while trying to pick up dog poop from the kitchen floor. Or when the smoke detector goes off. Because your casserole (that none of your children will eat tonight) is burning. And you have an important meeting at 8 a.m. tomorrow that you haven't prepped for. And someone else still needs help with their homework. More more more more good-mom performance is needed, and Team Kid is totally tapped out.

In the yawning chasm that opens up when Team Kid stops running its magnificent plays, Inner Baby parts suddenly spring forth—and then quickly, quickly (there's no time to waste!), a few bold players from Team *What About Mom?!* move in to the rescue (we will have no sadness here!). Resentment, Anger, and Fuck-it find their way onto the open field, loading the bases and getting ready for action. There's a lot of vulnerability in the air, but Team *What About Mom?!* has no appetite for your Inner Baby's tears or fears. Guess who makes their way up to bat? Your Blamer is right there, scratching her jock and chewing and spitting, ready to hit a freaking grand slam. These parts aren't thinking about protecting your child's vulnerability so much as they're thinking about YOU. Your Bad Mom parts have shown up to save you. Finally! Someone's got their eyes on Mom for one meager, paltry minute, and the ball is hit and the crowd goes wild.

Only, it's kind of a vicious crowd, like at a football match in England when the home team starts hating on their star player (you soccer fans remember what happened to poor David Beckham), and before you know it, the crowd turns on Mom's own players. In the dugout, Guilt is tackling Anger, Resentment is clobbering your Anxious part, and the Blamer is screaming at your partner, who has been enjoying an actual baseball game on the actual TV this whole time while your own inner teams have been tearing you apart from the inside.

Components of the Loop

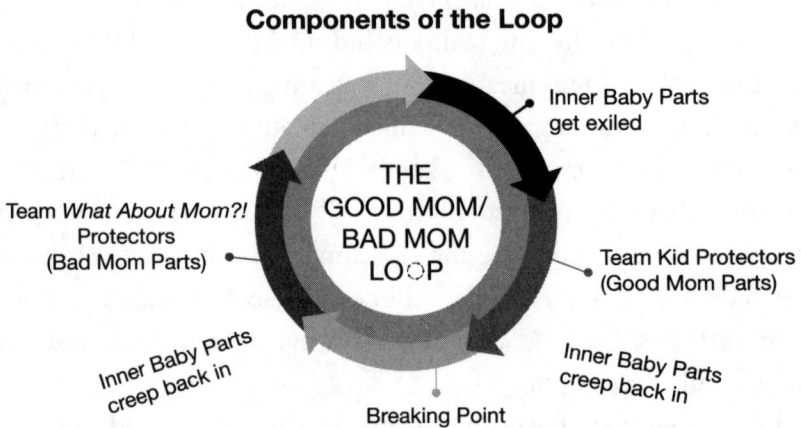

Team *What About Mom?!* exists to help Mom escape and to bring her relief and soothing. These protectors feel your Inner Baby parts, and they don't want your unmet needs to come alive and take over. They start looking for a way to release pressure (as in finally fucking letting yourself just YELL the curse words you've been biting back) or deaden the painful stimulus (as in knocking back a G&T with lunch). Team *What About Mom?!* has a thick playbook full of creative strategies for soothing and relief. However, most of those strategies result in some fallout or backlash or some kind of relational damage. Team *What About Mom?!*

parts make moves designed to get what they want right now; they're here to stop the pain, and they don't care about collateral damage.

Failure

Components of the Loop

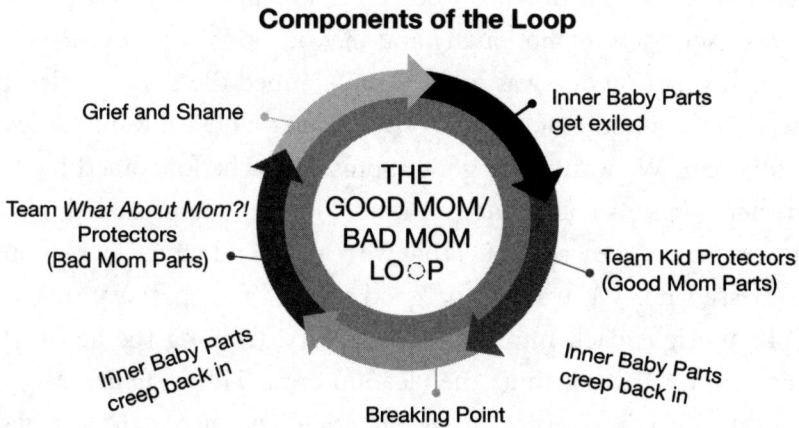

Grief and Shame

Inner Baby Parts get exiled

Team *What About Mom?!* Protectors (Bad Mom Parts)

THE GOOD MOM/ BAD MOM LOOP

Team Kid Protectors (Good Mom Parts)

Inner Baby Parts creep back in

Inner Baby Parts creep back in

Breaking Point

When you feel like a bad mom, like you've failed or been selfish, it can seem like there's no hope for repair or redemption. Your Inner Critic and Perfectionist unleash their judgment internally and bathe you in a steady flow of negative self-talk and self-recrimination. Shame and grief can completely take over the system and bring some of your more extreme parts out of the shadows, like your Panic, your Destroyer, and in some cases your Suicidal part. These parts show up when everything feels like it's on fire. Without enough support from outside or inside, these parts can stage a coup (blend with you) and totally block access to your source of internal wellness and regulation (your Inner Mom). When that happens, you no longer feel any sense of calm or confidence, and there's no courage or connectedness to draw on as you move forward in your day. In moments like these, you need to receive care and attention from a nonjudgmental, warmhearted, and receptive human who can help hold your despair respectfully so that maybe a little unblending can occur. IFS is so full of hope when it comes to these very hopeless parts. They are, after all, just parts of you—not all of you. And you do have an Inner Mom in there who can provide loving care to your distressed parts in ways they never knew possible.

Guilt and overwhelm are the bread and butter moms eat with every meal. We get down on ourselves for how we yelled again or how we shut down emotionally and met our kids with icy silence or got high when no one was looking or slammed the door and left the house in the middle of a hard conversation—and we want things to be different. We want to be good moms. We ache for something that isn't here—a sense of feeling connected, loved, or appreciated; a wish for closeness and ease; a belief that we're still good moms even though we messed up. We want to be good moms, and that Wanting part hooks us right back into our vulnerability, tripping the alarm that calls Team Kid back in as the cleanup crew. *I'll try harder. Maybe I can keep from ever screwing up like that again. I just need to be more disciplined.* The whole freaking loop begins again.

Self-recrimination and guilt become a lifestyle for moms who chase their tails, seeking redemption with over-the-top compensation-style mothering that exhausts and depletes them, triggering a need for relief or novelty or some goddam peace. We get completely blended with our Good Mom and Bad Mom parts, perpetuating a cycle of "goodness" while trying to clean up after "badness."

Interrupting the Loop

You can do something different.

To stop the brutal battles, we need to surrender into the sadness that's here. Your breaking point could be a moment of acceptance instead of destruction. It could have a feeling of softness more than self-blame. Grief more than shame. It's only in this painful spot—where the old reactive patterns appear once again, uninvited—that new self-compassionate patterns can be intentionally invited.

These are some of the most difficult, defeating moments in mother-hood. And sometimes they happen every single day. Having a rela-tionship with your parts gives you a new superpower—the ability to be *with* overwhelm instead of being in it. If you can be with the con-tents of what's overwhelming you, knowing there are tender Inner Baby parts aching with fear, sadness, and longing, you can start to mother those parts. You can give yourself incredible relief AND reg-ulate your nervous system just by noticing them, naming them, and validating their existence. Slow down a tiny bit and get curious. Turn toward this little-girl pain, not away from it. And from that slightly slower place, with one hand touching your own tenderness, you can speak to your children from a different place. You can speak for your parts (*I'm feeling overwhelmed right now and need a moment to help myself*) rather than from them (*Can you just shut up about the cookie?! You're driving me crazy!*).

If you are able to intervene with some Inner Mom energy as you're nearing your breaking point, you're teaching an old dog some very fancy new tricks. You're teaching your ingrained, reflexive, autonomic Good Mom parts that they can let go, maybe just for a minute. You're introducing a new resource into your system that communicates *safety*. You're acknowledging your Inner Baby parts enough to change the energy in your system.

✳ When your Inner Baby parts are seen and validated even just a little, the felt sense of urgency and desperation comes down a notch.

You're communicating this:
My needs get to exist too. My experience matters.
There's an Inner Mom onboard now, and so your Bad Mom parts don't have to pull out the big guns of Panic, Rage, or Suicidal ideation to help you get out of overwhelm. They can lean into your Inner Mom instead. Over time, with your continued respect and attention, your

parts will trust that you will keep showing up, nonjudgmentally and compassionately. Rather than needing to get you the hell out of over-whelm, they can feel held. By you. In the overwhelm.

It's not comfortable. You do have to feel it to heal it, as cheesy as that sounds. You can't edit a document if it isn't open. So, it's here at your breaking point, when the document is open, where long-standing patterns can either be reflexively passed forward to the next generation, or they can be reconsidered and healed in the warmth of your Inner Mom. Cracking the code—and coming to recognize that your system is predictable—gives you new choices.

PART TWO

Healing

Chapter 7

There Is Nothing Wrong with You

This morning's breakfast disaster sent you over the edge again, all because of a spilled bowl of cereal (organic, fruit-juice sweetened, of course). Now it's nighttime and you're lying in bed, replaying every harsh word you said to your kids, wondering what kind of crap mother you've become.

Here's what we want you to know: You don't have to become a different person or stop having the feelings you have. Healing your parts means something entirely different: meeting your emotions with openness and genuine interest. When you listen to the parts of you that are Scared and Angry, you stop feeling so alone inside. The pieces start to come together.

Healing isn't the same as curing. It doesn't necessarily mean the end of hurting; sometimes it means you feel your hurt even more deeply. It's about engaging with your wholeness, being receptive to all that's there, and responding with kindness. In IFS terms, healing happens when your Self—your Inner Mom—shows up for your parts.

Healing your internal parts is no different from working on relationships in the outside world. It's ongoing and dynamic, existing on a continuum that has no end point. There are many, many layers of emotional experience that make up the fabric of our relational connections with our children and our partners, with friends, family of origin, and, as it turns out, with our own parts.

It isn't a one-and-done interaction that creates depth and trust. It's the repeated cycle of showing up, listening, caring, laughing, crying, messing up, and trying again that builds real connection and teaches us who we are together. The goal in relating with our parts is the same goal we have in relating with our kids: We nurture them through their development, through awkward, challenging stages, and into smoother, easier times, riding the waves and adjusting our responses to what's needed now, and now, and now. We bring to motherhood a field of maternal energy that perceives, receives, and holds whatever is happening for our kids. That field of maternal energy is a healing space, and you can tap into that same magic to support yourself.

Maybe this idea of healing as a self-initiated, long-term endeavor feels disappointing. It would be great if you could just have a singular orgasmic healing moment with your parts and walk off into the sunset, good as new, never to fall into the pain of your shame or grief again. *Sigh*.

Healing *can* bring huge dynamic leaps forward and sometimes does move us at the speed of light into happier and healthier territory. But there's a more ordinary, subtle, everyday kind of healing that grows over time. It's quiet, but it's solid and real. This everyday healing comes from being in relationship with your Mom Parts and treating yourself with respect. This kind of healing is intimate and slow growing—and is simultaneously a massive, antipatriarchal cultural paradigm shift. It's built on this wholesome recognition:

✳ Moms have lots of different parts.
✳ All your parts make sense.
✳ All your parts need care.
✳ There's nothing wrong with you.

When Your Breaking Point Becomes Your Breakthrough

Healing is needed wherever there's an injury. Parts of you have come to believe that you're a bad mom, that you're not good enough, or that you're broken and unworthy. That pain is revealed at your break-ing point, when you can no longer manage all the stimulation and demands that are sucking away your life force, you can't suppress your own Inner Baby parts, and you fucking crack.

Out come your Bad Mom parts, dragging your good name through the dirt, doing damage, and stirring up shame and grief. Now there you are—hurting and injured, standing alongside your hurting, injured kids.

And from here, you either go into serious cleanup mode—trying to manage away and hide and exile everything awful that just happened—or you try a more relational approach with yourself. You start treating yourself like you make sense, and you start noticing your parts and inquiring into them, with the assumption (this is the big change maker here) that *every single one of your parts is trying to help you.*

All of a sudden, you're on your own team. Whichever part from whichever team is ruling inside of you, you recognize it as a home-town hero, and you know for certain that beneath all its bluster, it makes sense. You know it's attempting to help protect your Inner Baby, whom it has assessed to be fragile and doomed. You approach it with kindness, or at least interest. This type of healing is an invisi-ble internal process that will completely transform how you relate to yourself and how you respond to your children.

✳ Every single one of your parts is trying to help you.

Building Relationships Inside of You

Having a relationship with your parts allows you to speak about your internal experience and your behavior with clarity. When you understand yourself, you feel better. Understanding yourself includes knowing how you feel emotionally and then connecting those feelings to what's happening in your body, and to the words coming out of your mouth.

Yes, you still have parts. Yes, your parts still react and sweep you into old beliefs and emotions. But you have more curiosity and respect for what they're doing and why they're doing it. You're less reactive to their big emotions and beliefs. You make sense to yourself. You trust yourself more.

Building a relationship requires getting to know someone and letting them get to know you. Parts are like people, so the same relational rules apply inside as they do outside. Just like you would inquire with a new acquaintance, you start by being curious with your parts. You can ask them the same kinds of questions you'd ask a new neighbor you're just getting to know.

JOURNAL

Try getting to know a part by interviewing it this way:

Tell me about yourself. What job are you doing in my life? Do you like your job? How long have you been doing that job?

When you show up with curiosity, parts can feel your sincerity and your presence.

Where do you hang out (in my body)? What kind of beliefs do you have? What are you really struggling with right now? Which of my other parts do you dislike most?

When protectors feel enough connection and trust *inside of you*, they start to share more about their beliefs, hopes, and fears.

How are you trying to help me? What are you afraid would happen if you stopped doing what you're doing? What are you most hoping for?

It's through this sharing inside that you locate the root of your pain and learn what really and truly is making you suffer. Usually, it's a toxic and inaccurate belief about yourself in some way being bad or unworthy of love and belonging (Inner Baby stuff). Those areas of shame and grief can be held and healed now—'cause guess what: You're a capable and resourced adult! You may not feel like you are, but compared to when you were small, when your protector parts first formed, you have incredible power and strength to bring to the game.

Using the Power You Already Have

As mothers, we are practiced at loving our children. We've been doing that for a while now. We've stretched our patience and our caretaking prowess to new heights, widths, and depths, and we're kind of badass. (At least when we aren't super triggered or depleted.)

We have this wondrous opportunity to access and harvest some of the regenerative, life-giving love that we cultivated for our kids— and we can use it for ourselves now too. The maternal love, patience, and connection that have expanded inside of us are now free-floating in our systems and available to reuse, recycle, and repurpose in any manner that we choose.

This is a HUGE gift that motherhood brings us—more love onboard to work with. And the more we access that love for our own use, in the form of kindness, patience, and compassion for ourselves, the bigger the reservoir grows. We discover that we have more of all those resources to give to our kids by virtue of being generous with ourselves. More means more.

Your IFS Tool Kit: Three Ways to Transform Your Inner World

Now that you understand that your parts make sense and are trying to help you, let's explore some practical tools that can support your parts-exploration. These three IFS techniques will give you concrete ways to improve your relationship with your internal world.

IFS Tool 1: Unblending—Creating Space Between You and Your Intense Emotions

What it is: Unblending means stepping back from overwhelming feelings so you can see them clearly, like taking off glasses that were all fogged up.

Why it matters: When you're "blended" with a part, you become that emotion completely. You don't just feel angry—you ARE angry. Unblending enables you to say, "I have an angry part," instead of "I'm so mad at you!"

How it works: We all know that blending means mixing things together. We put kale and bananas and other ingredients into the blender to mix them to such a degree that the ingredients become indistinguishable from each other. You don't want to taste the kale? No problem! There are banana molecules all over it now, and you can't tell kale is even in there.

When it comes to your internal world being blended, you might only be experiencing your Angry part the same way your smoothie screams BANANA when it hits your taste buds. But you still have other parts that exist despite the prominence of the Angry one. Your Angry part is doing the same kind of work as the banana, masking something that's hard for your system to swallow—in this case, fear or hurt. But most important of all, you still have an Inner Mom that's alive and well-resourced hidden underneath the Angry part that has become adhered to your system in a very blended way.

When we talk about "unblending" in IFS, we're talking about separating out individual parts of you that may have merged with all your other internal ingredients to create a generalized emotional flavor. And that flavor is the one that takes over your nervous system. Unblending is an intentional way of disidentifying with your parts—effectively pulling the banana back out of the smoothie so that you can behold the kale in all its distinct glory. It's about peeking under the Angry part and witnessing the fear or the hurt it protects.

What being unblended sounds like:

- "When you left a mess on the counter this morning, a part of me got really irritated, and that's why I snapped at you."
- "I have a part that's afraid to have another child and really wants to call it one and done because of how hard pregnancy was the first time."
- "Part of me gets scared when you don't respond to my texts—and that's the part that did the yelling and crying."

IFS refers to this as "speaking for, not from, your parts." Kids like it when moms do this. Partners like it too.

Unblending happens on a spectrum. It's not all-or-nothing. If you can tell that you have an activated part, congratulations—you're already a little unblended. If you're able to notice it, and feel or hear what it reports, you have unblended from it even more. You're interacting with it. It's at least a little bit separate from you. Nice work. You're having a relationship with this part of you now and beginning to show it who you are: a resource that it can use going forward. Rather than your part running the show, you're now available for support. There's a YOU here with your part now.

Find our guide for unblending ("When You Need to Unblend from a Part") in chapter 12.

IFS Tool 2: Befriending—Building Trust and Connection with Your Parts

What it is: Befriending means getting curious about your parts and treating them with the same kindness you'd show a friend who's struggling.

Why it matters: Your parts have been trying to protect you, often for years. They need to know you're on their side before they'll relax and trust you to handle things differently.

How it works: Befriending is about respecting your parts and earning their trust. You're befriending your parts when you start to offer even very basic acceptance to a previously unknown or rejected part (like Rage, a Suicidal part, or Panic). Befriending can become an internal love affair that includes intimate expressions from your Inner Mom to parts of you, creating incredible tapestries of connection, compassion, tenderness, love, and appreciation. These tapestries can include even the parts that might've once scared or disgusted you.

Mariah, a long-term client who became deeply invested in healing her Inner Baby, described befriending in her system: "I'm a really good companion to myself now in the hardest moments, in the most mundane moments, and in the really good moments." Mariah has cultivated the ability to stay with her parts, not abandon herself or betray her own vulnerability. She knows and trusts herself and is there as "a soft place to land" when her parts are struggling.

What befriending sounds like: Speaking to yourself, you might say, "Wow, you made breakfast, packed lunches, got the dog taken care of, put yourself together, AND stayed friendly on the drive to school this morning. You're incredible. I so admire your capability and your commitment to being kind, even when you're feeling stressed."

Or...

"I know you didn't get anything you needed this afternoon. You took care of everyone else, and you felt so freaking irritated and exhausted. But I like the way you validated your Inner Baby and let her know you felt her and saw her, even when you had to ask her to keep waiting for your attention. That was new, and it made the day a little easier. You were a good mom to yourself and your kids."

Yes—you can say that to yourself. Out loud even. In the mirror, looking yourself in the eyes, if you're feeling really bold. Your parts could use that kind of validation.

IFS Tool 3: Unburdening—Helping Parts Release Old Pain and Limiting Beliefs

What it is: Unburdening helps parts let go of painful stories they've been carrying, like "I'm not good enough," or "I have to be perfect to be loved."

Why it matters: Sometimes parts get stuck carrying beliefs and pain from the past. When they can release these burdens, they return to their natural, more relaxed states.

How it works: Negative beliefs and burdens fall away organically as we unblend from and befriend our parts. Unblending and befriending can improve our lives dramatically. When we develop the capacity to witness the depth of our despair and fear and pain, some of it heals. And when we become courageous enough to allow others to witness the depth of our despair and fear and pain, more of it heals.

Sometimes on our healing journey, we encounter deeply wounded parts that are stuck in time, mired in what feels like intractable old pain that doesn't subside or relax with our own witnessing. These parts need support from an external source to get out of the past, out of whatever scene or memory they're stuck in.

An IFS therapist can help parts unload their sticky, toxic beliefs and heal wounds of unworthiness, badness, and shame through an unburdening process. Unburdening can happen bit by bit, and it can also happen spontaneously. There is an unburdening protocol for which IFS therapists receive rigorous training. In this process, therapists help parts locate where they're holding burdens in the body, what precisely they're holding, and why they're holding it. Witnessing and validation are heaped upon the suffering part. Then, if and when the part is ready, there's an invitation to let the painful burden go. People often release their burdens into one of the elements—air, earth, fire, water—or by some other inspired means. And when the burden is gone, parts are restored to their natural states, which tend to be playful, connected, calm, and relaxed.

While it's common to think of unburdening as the "goal" of IFS, it's really important to us that you know healing happens all the time, with or without unburdening.

It is our belief and our experience that improving your relationship with your parts is 100 percent where it's at, and relationships don't have an end point—they're ongoing, interactive, and dynamic. Unburdenings are like orgasms—big, powerful payoffs. But healing exists within a long, meaningful, ongoing back-and-forth relationship. Our advice: Lean into cultivating and nurturing that meaningful space between you and your parts, rather than looking for the climax.

HELENA'S STORY

Helena is a divorced mom who got remarried a year ago and is raising her fourteen-year-old daughter in a blended family. She described her internal struggle over how much freedom to give her daughter.

"The other afternoon my daughter and her friend were out at a carnival event in our town, and it was starting to get dark, which made me nervous. There's been gang activity in that part of town recently, including a shooting at another family event where someone was fatally injured. I just get so nervous having her out on a weekend night when I know people are partying and crowds are getting wilder than usual."

Helena was able to identify an Anxious part who was feeling preoccupied with tracking her daughter and monitoring her safety. When she went inside, she noticed her racing heart and a feeling of helplessness about not being able to keep her daughter safe.

"I started imagining her getting hurt, and I got panicky. I texted her and told her I was on my way to get her. She was really mad at me! She and her friend were having a good time, and they wanted to stay and ride more rides. I had a part that was really determined to hold my line. That part made me kind of angry and unwilling to bend."

Helena closed her eyes and felt her Angry part in the center of her body, and as she slowed down and brought curiosity to it, she became aware of how much fear that part was holding. She described her fear as "terror and helplessness" and got tears in her eyes as she allowed herself to experience it more fully. Her energy quieted, and she started to feel some compassion for her Anxious and Angry parts, and her body relaxed a little as she stayed with it, bringing more curiosity.

"The other girl's mom was fine with them being out at the carnival at night. She was texting me too, and she was pushing for letting them stay. She didn't seem anxious at all, and so I felt kind of judged then, and I had another part show up that was really mad at me for being so anxious. This part was more of an Inner Critic, and it was on my case for being a helicopter mom. I could hear it saying how much my daughter has already had her wings clipped from living through COVID, and that I should be encouraging her to take more risks and to be more independent. I started feeling like there's no way to win. If I let my Anxious part lead, I'll keep her safe, but she'll hate me and she'll never learn to survive out there alone. Plus, the other mom will judge me. If I let her stay out in the dark, she'll grow more self-confidence and maturity, but I'm also leaving her in an unsafe situation where something really bad could happen. I'll never forgive myself if something bad happens to her. I can't lose her. I just started to feel totally overwhelmed and like I couldn't win. I texted her back and said, 'Fine. Stay all night. I'll see you in the morning.' I definitely felt a Fuck-it part jump in and basically throw in the towel on worrying and trying to keep her safe. I stopped responding to her texts at all. I was feeling like no matter what I did as a mom in that moment, I'd be losing her, and I was just over it. But then a few minutes later, I started to feel embarrassed and guilty for having such a big reaction. I think I kind of scared my daughter when I ghosted her."

Helena was describing reaching her breaking point. She had different Mom Parts that opposed each other as they all aspired to protect her child in ways that had very conflicting strategies. Her Anxious part wanted to get her kid to safety and had a lot of underlying fear and sadness. That Anxious part was fighting against her Inner Critic—who was mad at her for not supporting her kid's independence. Helena's system registered the noise from those polarized parts (along with a feeling of being judged by the other mom and being disliked by her daughter) as impossible to metabolize, and she erupted.

Being a good mom had become impossible, according to her Inner Critic. She reached overwhelm, where she was beyond her capacity and yet the demands on her were still coming. No decision and no action would be the right one. A sense of failure was looming. And so that's when her Fuck-it part swooped in to the rescue and took her offline completely. Fuck-it pulled her out of mom mode and into a different psychological space, where she was off the hook for pleasing others and solving complicated problems that her system had determined to be unsolvable.

Helena was taken over by her grief as she touched into her lack of control. "I'm so afraid I won't be able to protect her and that something bad will happen to her." As her tears moved through her, she started feeling more compassionate toward herself. "I can see now that any choice I made would have been coming from a good place."

The Benefits of Putting Yourself First

Anything you want to be able to offer your child you have to give freely to your own Inner Baby. Lots of moms think otherwise—that they can be fantastic, generous, patient moms while hating on themselves—but it's just not true. When you don't know how to listen to yourself, find your innocence, or offer compassion to your own Inner Baby, you will quickly hit a wall in motherhood. Your kids will see right through you. They'll call your bluff, and you'll smash headfirst into your breaking point over and over again under their watchful eyes.

✳ If you want to improve your mothering, become better at loving yourself.

Focusing on your own parts is a direct path to being a better mom; identifying your protectors and helping them relax is the key to improving your mental health. When your protectors are relaxed, you become calmer and wiser. You feel grounded in Inner Mom energy and have access to some calmness, confidence, clarity, or compassion. In this more relaxed state, your heart is open and you're in connection mode. Your Inner Mom does the mothering from your Self, rather than from your parts—and this is a different way to define and understand "good" mothering.

It's not so much about avoiding conflict, never making mistakes, or raising perfect children. Mothering from your Self and orienting around your warm, caring Inner Mom energy creates trust and confidence. You feel *in* your integrity. You have more resilience because you know how to understand and talk productively about whatever shit show just happened, and you can separate your own triggers from what your kids are truly needing.

When your protector parts are relaxed, you stop handing down the BS that your parents handed down to you, which was handed down to them because everyone was so freaking traumatized and in such survival mode that they didn't have the option to grow and heal like you do now. Our ancestors helped get us here, to this place and time where we have the benefits and the burdens of all their toiling and suffering—and we have more time and space and freedom with which to approach our lives.

We can read books like this one and apply new healing modalities to our inner worlds. We can thank our ancestors for getting us here— and then we can start sorting through all the crapola they dumped on us. We can be the cycle breakers. When you know your parts, you can heal them. You can't be a cycle breaker if you aren't in the trenches with your parts, learning where the wounds are and providing care.

The End of Mommy Wars

Moms are supposed to love motherhood, and when they don't, they're left to wonder what's gone wrong. They look around at all the other moms who *seem fine*, and they start to wonder, *Is it just me? No one's talking about not liking being a mom. Are the other moms fronting? Or is there something wrong with me?* When mothers learn to work with their parts instead of against them, something beautiful happens—not just internally, but in how they relate to other mothers.

Motherhood can become a performance, designed to make Mom look competent and...morally superior. She buys the right stuff, makes the right moves, says the right things, and tries to mimic what she's perceiving to be good mothering. In the meantime, all her Mom Parts are going fucking wild inside her, especially when her baby won't stop crying, or her toddler keeps running away from her, or her teen is flunking out of algebra, or her adult child can't get a job. Her Good Mom parts inhibit and hold back her shame and her grief and try desperately to keep doing motherhood right. Her Bad Mom parts start clawing for a little bit of relief or peace or empowerment for herself when she feels like all she does is self-sacrifice.

Moms' Inner Critics can be brutal. Other moms can also be vicious. It's the stay-at-home moms against the working moms. The breastfeeders against the bottle-feeders. The co-sleepers feeling superior to the cry-it-outers. Moms of college-bound teens looking down their noses at moms of kids heading to trade schools. Polarized mommy wars shape moms' ideas about maternal norms and acceptability and how to fit in with the pack and how to be the *best* mom possible, playing on our innate fight-or-flight instincts and stirring up all kinds of conforming and rebelling Mom Parts within the mommy social milieu.

But it doesn't need to be that way. When moms are supported in being real with each other, in letting their vulnerability be known and seen, the climate changes immediately to one of appreciation and encouragement. Moms need each other. We need the crazy experiences we're having to be normalized, and we need to feel seen and accepted by people who understand us and know how hard we're working. Other moms who are going through all the same massive changes and feeling an uprising of the same intense parts can provide powerful validation to smooth our feathers and drop us into a calmer, steadier state.

But what happens more often is that moms show up in social circles looking for validation and instead wind up on the giving-and-receiving end of "mom shaming," swimming alongside one another in a sea of mom guilt. The inter-mom dynamics might superficially be about seeking and offering support to each other, but those dynamics often hide an unspoken element of competition and cruelty. It's hard to believe how rough it is out there in the mommy social scene, but it really is. In a society where authentic motherhood, complete with all its Mom Parts, isn't acknowledged or supported, moms with big, painful feelings turn against themselves and each other. You've heard the saying "Hurt people hurt people," right? Moms feel like they're failing a little at everything, and they compare themselves, hoping to gain ground somewhere, even if it's at another mom's expense.

In our group work with Mom Parts, we've seen this mommy war dynamic disappear in minutes, when moms are given the language and permission to share about their parts and their shame and they hear their experience echoed all around them. *You feel rage too? You don't always like being a mom either?* They become courageous and compassionate. The competitive, performance-based mom stuff slips away, and genuine connections grow. Speaking in Mom Parts language changes the tone between moms from one of competition and one-upping to one of admiration and affection.

Mistakes Are Allowed in Motherhood

Taking incredible, loving care of yourself is the most empowered form of rebellion. At a time when women are experiencing heightened misogyny and new restrictions on their bodily autonomy from political forces, it's more important than ever to love and value yourself. It's more important than ever to make sure you are prioritizing the care of your vulnerable parts. When we don't feel safe outside, we can still create safety within our own internal family of parts.

> ✷ No one can stop you from loving yourself. Taking incredible, loving care of yourself is the most empowered form of rebellion.

Self-compassion is a gift you can be liberal with—and you don't need anyone else's permission or involvement. Making sure your Inner Baby knows you love her is some of the most awesome spiritual work you can do in this lifetime, and it's work that has gigantic ripple effects. Addressing your unmet needs with respect and reverence—the ones from childhood and the ones that are cropping up now, in real time—will change how you operate in the world. True empowerment comes from helping your parts relax and rest in your internal resources. There is no more valuable aspiration than to heal yourself.

As we move forward, there are a few assumptions we'd like you to try on. Assuming the following to be true will give you a head start with your healing. (Plus, these things really are true—you just might not know it yet.)

- Your parts are always trying to help you (even the funky ones).
- At the core, you are innocent.
- You are worthy of love and of living a good life.
- Mistakes are allowed.

Let's say it again—together, this time: Mistakes are allowed. This is a formative time for you, not just for your child. You are allowed to be someone who is learning and developing. There is no other way it can be. This time is for you just as much as it's for your child.

✳ This is a formative time for you, not just for your child.

The Truth About Self-Compassion

To offer yourself kindness and to genuinely feel self-compassion, your protectors have to chill out. Most of us have a strong Inner Critic who blocks kindness from flowing inward. We know in IFS that you cannot override an Inner Critic or any other protector part who believes they must continue doing their job (in the IC's case—self-punishing, self-blaming, and self-recriminating) to keep you safe. Protectors have to be befriended if you are going to create a nontoxic internal environment. This means getting curious about your Inner Critic and helping it see there's another way.

Perfection is bullshit. Trying to perform your way into good mental health doesn't work. Let self-compassion be your new goal and your highest ideal. Self-compassion is sexy, strong, confident, inclusive, flexible, health giving, and contagious. In a world where there is so little we can control, self-compassion is the surest thing and the best medicine.

You can't fake this. Like all children, your parts are bullshit detectors, and they know when you genuinely feel compassion and when you're just going through the motions. Without your own friendship and compassion, you won't feel better. You'll continue to have protector parts running your show, perpetuating old patterns based on fear. If you want to change those patterns, your distressed parts need to genuinely feel your care and your interest. There are no shortcuts or ways around it. Parts are like kids—they don't thrive without their mom's love and interest.

Once childhood has passed, we cannot get our Inner Baby's unmet needs healed by others. We keep looking for external approval and love, believing that's what we need to feel whole and safe. External love and approval were exactly what we needed when we were small—but that's not what we need now, in adulthood. The only thing that will truly hit the spot now is internal acceptance and love. Self-compassion.

From Self-Attack to Self-Care: A New Way Forward

Going inside, identifying parts, speaking truths, and acknowledging our shame and our grief—these are powerful steps toward everyday healing. Quiet internal shifts that transform how we experience motherhood.

The source of your goodness as a mom is not located in all your hard work (although the amount of labor you do is awe-inspiring). Maternal goodness—the yummy stuff that really meets your kids' needs—comes from your Inner Mom. The meaningful substance that moms bring to the planet flows from resources cultivated in our own healthy brains and hearts. Kids benefit from our hard work, but they reap the greatest rewards from how we lend them our nervous systems through our intuition and ability to attune to their experience. They soak up what we pour into them and metabolize our energy into their own. They learn from our way of being with our parts and adapt their own way of being with their parts and other people's parts. When we feel safe, we share that feeling with our kids. When we know what it's like to feel held, we can truly hold others. When we make sense to ourselves, we can honor our kids' emotions and make sense of their wild parts.

Your relationship with your children is a live broadcast of the status of your relationship with yourself. That live broadcast shows you exactly where you're hurting and where you need care and support. And the right thing to do with that information is not to get down on yourself or beat yourself up. The right thing to do is to seek understanding (your parts make sense).

When you hit a rough patch, rather than moving into reflexive self-hate or self-improvement plans, try our approach. Right away, remember that you have an Inner Baby who is full of tenderness and also that you have an Inner Mom who can help her. Bring your Inner Mom closer to your tenderness. Let some curiosity lead the way, and trust that your parts have wisdom to share. Rather than condemning yourself or someone else, maybe your inner dialogue can go something like this:

Based on how I'm behaving, I must be hurting inside.

Ah, I'm hurting.

My Inner Baby parts are sad or scared or full of longing, and my protector parts are getting all stirred up, trying to make my pain go away.

I want to understand the story they're telling.

I'm going to go inside and see what they're saying and look for my Inner Mom to come and care for these parts.

I'm going to let my parts know that I understand they're trying to help.

There's more of me here now, to mother myself.

When you need healing, turn to the places you feel safest and most at home. When you're held in safety, there's more room to venture into the shadows and meet your grief and shame. Your grief and shame need you. They need your presence and your care, your witnessing and your validation. Many moms before you have found ways to feel held while they venture into the shadows within the context of their best friendships, through tending to their bodies with therapy, massage, nutritional support, medication, time in nature, time alone, silence, and more and more, through psychedelic-assisted psychotherapy, which has uniquely powerful healing potentials that "map onto IFS very well."[1]

✳ Your relationship with your children is a live broadcast of
the status of your relationship with yourself.

Remember that morning with the spilled cereal? The words you can't take back, the shame spiral that visited you while you were lying in bed? Let's revisit that scene through the lens of what you've learned thus far.

What if, instead of lying in bed replaying every harsh word through your Inner Critic and wondering what kind of mother you've become, you tried something different?

What if you got curious about the parts that showed up that morning? First, you might start by asking your Inner Critic what she's afraid of and how she's trying to help you. Ask her if she can feel your genuine interest in her concerns. Maybe that will help her soften enough to allow you to notice there might also be a Resentful part who has been juggling too much for too long. Let her know you get it! She does overextend herself, and it makes sense that she's fed up. Maybe there's a Perfectionist part who has impossibly high standards for how mornings should go—who was wanting a smooth beginning to the day and not the chaos you encountered that made you late for work again. Maybe there was a Scared part underneath it all, worried that the spilled bowl of cereal and the milk seeping under the cabinets meant you were failing somehow.

Instead of the late-night shame spiral, what if you said, "I see you, Resentful part. You've been holding so much. And you, my Perfectionist—you want everything to be just right because you want to prevent me from hurting. You both make complete sense." What if you let your Inner Mom hold space for all of it—the Inner Critic, the milk all over the floor, you losing your cool and lashing out? What if you let yourself cry a few tears and appreciated your parts for helping you hold so many loose ends together in the midst of such a challenging day?

This shift from shame to self-compassion isn't just about one morning or one messy spill. It's about changing how you relate to yourself.

You can take beautiful care of yourself, whether or not the world shows up for you. You have the power to care for all your parts, even the ones who feel hopeless or enraged. As your parts feel better understood by you, things start to make more sense inside, and the internal chaos quiets down. You naturally start experiencing more curiosity toward the many paradoxical and heroic parts of yourself. That curiosity opens up your heart and connects you to your deeper pain and fear—and you're able to be more present with them now. There's more compassion for your own suffering and some space to feel your grief. Pressure is released. You feel better. You realize you can trust yourself, even with all your undomesticated parts. And your formerly feral, untamed parts grow to trust you. Your Inner Baby is put in the care of your Inner Mom.

No matter what distorted, critical, or convoluted messages you're receiving from outside, hear this: You are the planet's most powerful influencer. Your wellness really matters. Collectively, we rely on you to pass on the wisdom of your nervous system to the next generation. Through you, humans learn who they are. Through you, small beings come to know their own parts and their own Inner Moms. Through you, they absorb implicit knowledge of how to regulate themselves so they can bring their gifts to this world and not start more wars or perpetrate more violence. For them to be well, we need you to feel seen and safe and loved. The more you thrive, the better we all fare. Mothering is the heart of our humanity.

Chapter 8

The First Step to Transformation

Maria stared at her sixteen-year-old daughter's bedroom door, still closed at 2 p.m. on a Saturday. Again. The dishes from last night's dinner—the ones her daughter had promised to wash—sat untouched in the sink. The laundry basket overflowed. And somewhere in that dark cave of a room, her once-chatty little girl was probably scrolling TikTok, ignoring the world.

Maria felt a familiar surge of anger. *She doesn't care about this family. She treats me like I'm invisible unless she needs money or a ride somewhere. I don't even know who she is anymore, and honestly? I don't think I like who she's becoming.*

The urge to bang on that door and deliver a lecture about responsibility was overwhelming. But then Maria remembered what she'd been learning about her parts—how her Angry part always showed up when she felt powerless, and how her Sad part carried all the hurt about losing connection with her daughter. She'd been trying to get to know these parts better instead of just letting them take over.

Instead of storming down the hallway, she sat on her couch and closed her eyes. *What's really happening inside me right now?* she asked herself. *What am I actually feeling underneath this Angry part?*

In that moment of stillness, she felt it—a deep ache in her chest that had nothing to do with dirty dishes and everything to do with missing her daughter. The anger was there, yes, but underneath it was grief for the close relationship they used to have. And though her grief wasn't easy to experience, it felt more honest than her anger, and she noticed herself relaxing and letting go of the tension in her jaw.

This simple question—*What's really happening inside me right now?*—is what we call "going inside" in IFS. It's the first step toward understanding the different parts of yourself that show up in challenging moments and learning how to care for them rather than being overtaken by them.

Going inside is shorthand for a process that involves pulling your attention away from external stimuli and turning it inward, often with your eyes closed, so that you can find and focus on exactly how your body is activated. Your body doesn't lie. It holds the charge and activation of everything you've been thinking, feeling, and believing. When you slow down long enough to notice and direct your interest toward yourself, the story of your experience—of your "parts"—becomes clearer.

The Art of Inner Listening

Going inside means getting quiet for a few minutes and paying close attention to yourself. It means noticing how your body feels, with all its aches and pains, buzzing energy, or maybe even the absence of sensation. It means paying attention to your thoughts, whether they are racing or distant. It means becoming aware of your emotions and welcoming each one. Most of all, it means getting curious.

Most moms don't ever do that. We think we don't have time and we don't know how, or maybe we're scared to slow down, even for a moment. Our attention is located outside of our bodies, on all the other people we're supporting, pretty much all the time. We're so busy making sure the gluten-free kid has the right bread on their sandwich and the basketball player has eaten more than just candy for lunch today that, once again, we forget to feed ourselves. We subsist on our kid's uneaten crust of GF bread, and when the raging headache hits and we start snapping at everyone, we feel bad for being such a grumpy mom. But when so little energy is allocated to the tending of our own personal experience, we cannot thrive. These pages offer explicit permission and encouragement to pay attention to your inner world. You may be very out of practice, but we're going to guide you back toward yourself in a way that doesn't require abandoning your family or completely remodeling your life. It starts with going inside.

Right now, we're asking you to turn inward, toward yourself. Show up in your own body for a little bit, noticing what thoughts you're thinking, the sensations you're feeling, and the emotions that are flickering through your awareness.

Hello there.

Maybe there's a moment to just pause here and take a luxurious, slow breath.

Yes, like that.

To welcome your parts, you have to be present for them.

Your Body Holds the Truth

Most of what happens to us is experienced somatically, in sensations, without words. So locating that information has to happen by *being with* it, in your physical body. To understand the dynamics of your system, you have to bring your attention to what's happening inside of you. This matters because emotional pain is always informational— it's your internal system's way of signaling that something needs care.

When you go inside, you begin to notice and listen to what's been stirred up, along with the story you're telling yourself about it. That story holds so much important information about the meaning your parts are making of triggering events. Within that story, you can hear what it is you are most afraid of and what it is you were really hoping for. Those hopes and fears capture the truth of your parts. And when you get down to the truth of your parts, you will ultimately uncover pain, as well as essential innocence and good intentions.

When you're hurting emotionally, it's an indication that something inside your body or psyche is injured. On a surface level, you experience those injuries as psychological symptoms like anger, depression, or anxiety. But deeper in your brain, at the neural site of the injury, you've made synaptic connections that correspond to fear, shame, loss, or some other kind of distress. If you've been in distress for a prolonged period of time, it's likely that your nervous system has learned how to survive your injuries, but not how to heal them. You get on the treadmill of life each day, and your parts move you through your tasks on autopilot, in exactly the way they already know how to. They keep doing the same thing that perpetuates your distress and your symptoms. Your past repeats itself here in the present.

❋ Protector parts help us manage and cope. They aren't so good at helping us heal.

❋ Healing requires vulnerability and change.

Curiosity Rewires Your Brain

For emotional injuries to heal, your brain has to do some rewiring; certain neural connections consistent with pain need to weaken, and neural connections associated with safety or wellness need to strengthen. To get your brain to change and heal, your focused attention is required. Focused attention is the primary ingredient of neuroplasticity (the ability of the brain to adapt and reorganize), and without it, you continue to operate in your familiar homeostatic patterns.

Another word for focused attention is "curiosity." Curiosity is a healing agent that brings in alertness, which primes your brain chemistry for focusing. It spotlights your interest on a target area, which further adjusts your brain chemistry, creating the necessary habitat for healing.

Staying Curious

You might be thinking this sounds like meditation—and you're partly right. But the IFS approach to going inside differs from traditional meditation in important ways. Many traditional forms of meditation aim to move the meditator into a state of "no mind," where there are no longer any thoughts and the individual's attention stays exclusively on the breath or on a mantra. Meditators are encouraged to let go of attachment to feelings and sensations, the goal being to arrive at greater calm and peace.

Going inside IFS-style is different. The intention is to pay *more* attention to your thoughts, feelings, and sensations, with heightened focus and curiosity. The curiosity you bring to your experience is the change agent that shifts you from being *blended* with your parts to *unblending* from them and beholding them with new eyes and a more open heart. When you're blended with your parts, it's impossible to have any curiosity about them—you just believe them and speak from them ("Those teachers don't understand what my kid needs; they're all incompetent") and agree with everything those parts are asserting ("You're being so difficult right now! Why can't you just cooperate?"). Your parts are dysregulated, and so are you. They're in protection mode, and so are you.

When you're unblended from your parts, you're able to listen to them with interest. You can make sense of what's happening for your parts, and you have the ability to provide support to yourself, in exactly the way you need it. You can speak *for* your parts rather than speaking from them. You're capable of connecting with yourself and with others.

✳ Curiosity is the doorway to healing. When you get curious about your parts instead of battling them or becoming them, everything changes.

By bringing interest to your body, an intimate inquiry starts to catch the attention of parts of you that need care. That quivery feeling in your stomach is no longer pushed to the wayside but is instead brought right into the center of things. Perhaps for the first time ever, the funky sensation in your belly is allowed to be here. Now, with your attentive presence, it is looked into rather than being ignored or rejected. As that belly quiver is given some time and space to express itself, more information starts to come. Connections to past quivery moments begin to surface, and now there is a story emerging, sometimes sprinkling in images and memories from long ago. As you stay with that quivery part, continuing to bring curiosity to it, you learn the truth of the part's experience, which may be rooted in past traumas, old losses, or childhood fantasies.

Your ability to stay open to whatever it is your parts have been holding and believing connects you to the central core of your psychological wiring. Your attention and presence are powerful instruments that can rewire your system and give you access to new resources. Listening to your parts helps you discover old, festering wounds that have never healed. While these old beliefs very likely aren't true anymore, they were the root cause of your protective parts' emergence. You became a Fixer for a good reason. You learned how to Rage because you had to. The voice of your Inner Critic has familiar overtones of critical voices from long ago.

When you listen to the story your parts are telling, you discover that your parts are wise. They may be undeveloped, and they may be causing big problems, but once you hear where they're originating from and why they do what they do, you come to realize that you absolutely make sense. Every part of you.

In general, our tendency is to stay focused outside, on what others are saying or doing, and then REACT to those stimulating external events in an effort to change them and defend ourselves. Going inside imposes a deliberate pause and a redirecting of your attention onto yourself. Most often we close our eyes when we go inside. Our focus shifts from outside to inside—but then what? These four questions can serve as your inner compass, guiding your attention in a way that leads to real understanding and relief:

The Four Questions: Your Inner Compass

When you go inside, let these questions guide your attention:

What's happening inside? Start by simply noticing. Scan your body for tension, heaviness, or any sensation that draws your attention. Don't analyze yet—just acknowledge what's there.

Where does this part live in my body? Get specific about the location and quality. Is it a tight band around your chest? A heavy stone in your stomach? A buzzing energy in your shoulders? The more precise you can be, the clearer your part becomes.

What triggered this part? Now listen for the story. What is this part of you afraid of or protecting you from? Stay present without judgment as it unfolds.

How can I be with this part in a helpful, caring way? This is where transformation happens. Ask your part what it needs. Sometimes it just wants to be heard. Sometimes it needs reassurance or a promise that you'll pay more attention to what it's protecting.

This simple step of going inside can be transformative. It can move you out of a defensive position of fight/flight into a state of greater calm and openness. It's an invisible gift you give to yourself. While others will benefit from your increased calm and openness, it truly is a process designed just for you, to access your own internal resources for the purpose of finding, focusing on, and feeling toward your own parts.

You deserve your own attention and good care. When you go inside in a thoughtful, deliberate way, chances are you will experience your inner world as more welcoming and hospitable. As you move toward your parts with genuine interest—even the parts that typically scare you—you'll notice yourself feeling more *confident* and *courageous* than before. And when you learn the story of how your parts are trying with all their might to help you, it's hard not to melt a little and feel some real *compassion* for the kid you used to be, who had to develop these big protectors to survive and to be loved.

It's our own care that our systems are starving for. Our own attention and interest can companion us regardless of the chaos that exists around us.

Welcoming Your Enemies

This might be the first time you've willingly met up with your protector parts. It often feels counterintuitive to suddenly start welcoming emotions and beliefs that you've been trying to get rid of for years, like Depressed or Blamer parts. These are parts of yourself you probably don't like. To turn toward them and ask them to come closer might seem really absurd and even kind of dangerous. But you really can talk to your parts. They like to be respected and inquired into. Moms worry that by giving their parts attention, they will be giving those parts permission to completely take over, as in:

If I acknowledge my Rage, won't it just get bigger?

There's truth to the fact that some of our parts are destructive, cause harm, or don't fit very well in our lives. But when parts of us exist, they legitimately need attention. When we ignore or suppress our parts, we're using internal force and energy to push them away. We're communicating a message that they're not welcome. If you find yourself pushing parts away or having to choose one part over another, you can bet there will be equal and opposite backlash somewhere inside of you.

We're in the habit of being harsh, even ruthless, with our unwanted parts and shoving them down with great force. It takes some serious retraining to begin orienting this new way, where we turn toward and get curious about our parts, listening with interest, even to the scary ones. It works well to approach your unsettled parts the same way you'd approach little kids who are having a hard time. Something like this:

Hey there, I see you're feeling upset and needing some attention. I'm here now, and I'm going to help.

You may be asking, "But what if I can't help?"

It takes repetition and time to trust that you have what it takes to help. Remember that most of what kids and parts need is a caring, supportive adult who can be present. You can do that. Ask your part,

What's going on? What are you afraid of?

You can speak directly to your parts like they're separate people. It works.

What are you worried would happen if you didn't show up and take over my body and mind like this?

Along with expressing interest in your parts, you can also ask them for things. You can be in a relationship with them and negotiate. You can say to a Sad or Panicky part,

Can you turn your energy down inside of me so that my system doesn't feel quite so overwhelmed by you?

Or maybe to an Anxious or Angry part,

Would it be possible for you to wait in another room while I listen to my daughter tell me why she was so late getting home and never called?

Interacting with your parts respectfully like this will actually calm them down—not ramp them up. Engaging with them in a way that communicates that they matter makes them feel heard (again, like little kids who have been clamoring for attention). To do otherwise—to ignore them or exile them—is a form of neglect, abuse, and if you get down to it, internal violence that we perpetrate on ourselves. It's not friendly. Ignoring our feelings and our parts is common and condoned by our culture, but it's not helpful, and it increases the distress we feel. That can change now.

Start with just being interested.

GENEVIEVE'S STORY

Genevieve is a single mom who shares in therapy just how fed up and frustrated she feels with her six-year-old autistic son, who takes forever to eat breakfast, get his shoes on, and get in the car every morning for their long commute to school. She shares that she gets really pissed off at him and that she snaps. "He's not a baby anymore! He knows how to put his freaking shoes on! He must not care about me at all—or maybe he wants me to suffer. I think he's trying to show me that it's him who's in charge."

As Genevieve focuses inside, she can sense how she feels in her body, and she starts to listen more closely to this part of herself—how it feels and what it believes. With a little encouragement and direction, she starts to picture it almost like it's a separate being inside of her—one that she identifies as an Angry part. As she spends time describing and understanding her Angry part, she starts to notice that she also has a self-critical part that's edging its way in, this one saying, "If you were a better mom, you wouldn't get angry with your child. He's so little and you're all he has in this world. What's wrong with you?!"

This second part is now coming into focus, and Genevieve names it her Guilty part. She's beginning to see how those two parts—the Angry one and the Guilty one—create tension inside of her and make her feel awful as they battle against each other and try to silence one another.

Genevieve discovered these two parts in her system by slowing down and shifting her attention to her inner world. When she identified her Angry part who was stirred up from trying to get her slowpoke son out the door day after day, the entire spectrum of her experience became much more understandable. Of course she felt angry! Her nervous system was overloaded and full of intense feelings.

Naming her protectors as Angry and Guilty gave them an identity. Now Genevieve can see them, listen to them, and negotiate with them. She can start developing relationships with these parts that show up almost daily. They're no longer just a flood of emotions and impulses that surge inside her and take over her body, requiring her to either push them down or spew them out. They're separate from her, and they're something she can understand and speak for. Her Guilty part that was so tinged with self-criticism witnesses how she's making sense to herself now and starts to soften and fade a bit. "I'm a single parent with a high-needs kid. This is not easy. I think I need to go easier on myself and lower my expectations all around."

The next morning, when her son was moving slowly again, Genevieve felt her Angry part activate but was able to speak for it rather than from it: "Buddy, I'm feeling stressed about getting you to school on time. Can you help me by putting your shoes on now?" Her calmer tone helped her son focus, and they actually left on time—something that hadn't happened in weeks. The shift came from Genevieve better understanding herself and taking more time with her internal experience.

You can deliberately change only what you are aware of. As you bring more curiosity to your parts, you transform the tone of your internal dynamics from controlling and coercive to open and interested. It feels so much better. You can absolutely create sacredness in your parts when you make it a practice to acknowledge them, inquire into them, and visit them on the regular.

Welcoming your parts is incredibly validating and kicks off a new campaign of self-trust. When you consistently turn inward with curiosity rather than criticism, you're not just learning a technique—you're changing how you relate with yourself. You're moving from being at war with your inner world to being in partnership with it. And for mothers who spend so much energy caring for others, this simple practice of going inside becomes a radical act of self-care that ripples out and benefits everyone you love.

Chapter 9

The Healing Power of the Truth

Our protector parts are super invested in keeping us away from pain. We have reason to be grateful to them, because pain really stinks. But protectors see the world from a constrained perspective, which means they ignore or block out certain realities that they experience as pain-inducing. They steer clear of that triggering or undigestible stuff and stick with their tried-and-true path of controlling, fixing, blaming, and so on. And yet, those triggering aspects of your existence that get bypassed or buried by your protectors still exist. They're sitting somewhere, emanating reality, while your protectors skirt around them, avoiding contact for fear of what the truth would do to you. However uncomfortable it may be, the truth is critical to your health. When it's supported with care, it's what sets your compass to true north and aligns you with your own sense of trustworthiness.

✳ You have to encounter the truth and integrate it into your sense of reality in order to heal. You can't avoid the truth and expect to be well.

And the truth needs your care and companionship, especially when the truth brings up memories of pain or fear.

Linking Your Hidden and Visible Parts

Mom Parts Truths are simple, direct statements designed to speak to the parts of you that hold pain—and help them start expressing themselves. Truths are a bridge between your protectors and your vulnerabilities; they extend a lifeline to your tender parts who feel disliked and ostracized, and provide some powerful validation, encouraging them to feel more and say more.

Mom Parts Truths are not the only truths on earth, and they aren't meant to be mantras or aspirations. They're supportive talking points that either resonate or don't. They provide an opening for fleshing out your parts, and they're often just the tip of the emotional iceberg, with many more layers of truth nestled underneath. They're integral to unburdening. Here are the Truths that we offer to moms to support the building of a bridge between their protectors and their vulnerability.

TRUTHS

- Kids have really big feelings. (And babies cry a lot.)
- Nothing's perfect.
- Some things are out of my control.
- My child is still developing and is a work in progress. So am I.
- All kids go through painful times.
- Just because I don't like it doesn't mean there's something wrong.
- Sometimes my kid hurts my feelings.
- Sometimes I'm disappointed in my kid.
- Being a mom is really hard.
- I don't always like being a mom.
- I'm not getting my own needs met.
- I did the best I could.
- It's not fair.
- My kid really triggers my feelings of "I'm not good enough."

The truth comes with a story, and as you start to listen to that story, there's more context for all your wild emotions and reactions. You make more sense. Truths give you permission to feel how you feel and to say more about it. Your parts come into better focus and take shape outside of you. When you know your parts a little better—even the ones that scare you—that helps you understand more of their conflict and complexity. You really start to get what it is they've been wrestling with. Ready to try a Truth for yourself?

Just because I don't like it doesn't mean there's something wrong.

How does that land for you? Could it possibly be true that your parts might have an aversive reaction to something about your kid— and that it doesn't mean there's really something wrong? Lots of parts assume that because they feel bad, something terrible is happening. Not always so. This Truth can help Mom Parts calm down a little and take a second look—with some fresh curiosity.

Moving from Shame to Self-Compassion

Truths shift your inner dialogue from *There's something wrong with me* to *This is difficult for me.* From shame toward grief. From stuck to having choice.

Take a moment to let that sink in. That's a meaningful shift. Your Inner Critic takes notice and pauses its crusade. Your Inner Mom is made aware of how you're having a hard time, and she's inclined to care. Suddenly, the heat inside you cools, and the climate becomes more welcoming.

When your Inner Critic is less active, you feel less shame. You feel safer and more open. Improving your mental health has a lot to do with helping your Inner Critic calm down so that it stops shaming you and punishing you so much. Shame is the experience of believing you're bad. Shame identifies *you* as the source of badness and pretty much makes you out to be a hopeless case.[1] Healing from shame has to do with recognizing that a bad or a difficult thing happened *to* you, which opens up the possibility of recovery and repair. You're not a lost cause.

Acknowledging Truths helps you unblend and see your suffering with a little more objectivity. Light shines on this new realization: *I'm hurting. I need care, not punishment.* The Truths are a nudge in the direction of unshaming your struggle and restoring it to the simple thing that it is—a difficult experience.

Truths bring clarity. They sweep away the debris your protectors have created from all the extra trying, lying, and vying they've had to do to keep your fear or your pain in the shadows. When your Inner Critic is quieter, your system has a chance to let the Truth be spoken and to listen to it ring out and reverberate all around you. How about this one?

Sometimes my kid hurts my feelings.

What is it like to say it aloud? Truths deliver a stabilizing message to your Inner Critic—you are normal and understandable. The painful struggle you've been having in private, with some degree of shame or self-judgment, suddenly feels more workable. The fact that these words exist here on this piece of paper...

I don't always like being a mom.

...is an indication that someone else has had this thought or this feeling—proof that other moms feel this way too.

Truths communicate that it's okay to feel the way you feel. And if it's okay to feel the way you feel, then you're not bad, not a failure, but in fact, you're having a valid experience. You can relax a little. Exhale more fully. Allow your shoulders to drop another half inch. Something softens inside. Your tenderness emerges. You have new courage with which to greet your difficult, painful feelings. And maybe this Truth speaks to you then:

I did the best I could.

Oh. Compassion starts oozing out of your pores, all on its own. Self-compassion, no less. And a little grief too. Because your Truth might actually be this:

I'm not getting my own needs met.

Truths realign you with what you've always known in your core. It's always been there, but it's felt too dangerous or too triggering to other people for you to voice. You're vulnerable and hurting. That's all. Coming into contact with reality now and realizing that you're empowered enough to hold the truth's charge and stand behind it is revolutionary. You get to reclaim what you know to be true and allow it back into your awareness. You get to say the words and own them. Your heart starts to open, and compassion is here now, in the place where self-hatred or terror used to be.

MONIQUE'S STORY

Monique has a fifteen-year-old daughter in high school and a nineteen-year-old son who is away for his first year of college. She shares that her son has been mildly depressed for several years, and she's really worried about him now that she doesn't have eyes on him daily. She describes him as "sensitive" and "having a dark cloud that just colors everything" and then quickly adds, "It's my fault. I feel like a terrible mom for him being depressed. I must've done something wrong. I'm looking for a good therapist for him."

As she starts to slow down and go inside, Monique names her dominant Mom Parts as Scared, Responsible, Guilt, and Anxious. With a little encouragement, she does something novel: She shifts her attention away from her son's struggle and focuses on her own inner experience. She notices that in all her years of mothering, she's never really considered how she feels inside. She's been entirely fixated on "doing more, helping more, and taking care of them." Her Scared part is her most prominent part in this moment. She gets teary as she is able, for the first time, to acknowledge her own deep well of feeling that has been sitting unnoticed, just behind all her mom-related efforting. She lets her grief flow for a few minutes, beginning to recognize more than she ever has that her son is a separate person who has his own path ahead. There's only so much she can do to help him—and maybe she won't be able to take his depression away. She cries quietly, finally meeting the pain she hasn't wanted to confront. She can feel the depth of her love for him and starts to speak some truths that include her appreciation for herself.

"I've really been a good mom. I took good care of them. But I couldn't keep them from feeling their own pain and making their own mistakes."

By attending to her Mom Parts, Monique stops looping on a narrative that centers her as the one at fault. She feels more clarity about the limitations of what she can and can't do for her kids, and she's full of compassion and appreciation for her soft, loving mom heart. She places a hand on her heart and exhales, more calmness spreading through her body.

The Truth Can Feel Dangerous

Discovering and speaking a Truth can be the best thing ever, but sometimes the Truth is scary, unsettling, and disruptive to the values you so deeply want to embody and uphold. The Truth might feel like it blows up your facade and reveals weaknesses and injuries that you never wanted to be seen, things our culture says moms aren't supposed to think or feel, like this:

Sometimes I'm disappointed in my kid.

Your protectors have been working to mask and hide this Truth, but there's a new invitation here, an opening, maybe even a beckoning, to come closer to yourself, to start trusting what you've known in your gut all this time, even if you've fought hard to push it away. It's still been true. And now you have more strength, more capacity, and some encouragement (here from this book, and hopefully burgeoning out there in the mom zeitgeist) to trust yourself. To trust your parts. To believe you make sense.

The Cost of Hiding from Reality

When we're young and the Truth is too much for us to digest, our nervous system provides us with adaptive responses (i.e., parts) that help us navigate very complex dynamics. As kids, we can't really process truths that include not being wanted, not being safe, or not being loved—especially when acknowledging the truth puts us further in danger. An alcoholic mother who sometimes terrifies you? She's still the only mother you have and often is your only option for love and care. So you have to find a way to juggle the complicated task of hating her/watching your back/still needing her/wanting love and then seeking care when it looks safe to do so. That kind of shape-shifting takes a lot of intelligent parts who know how to grab the wheel and start steering in make-or-break moments.

But it's inherently conflictual and troubling to have parts who are adept at people pleasing and parts who are boiling with rage and parts who are terrified, all vying for attention and wrestling each other when they get stirred up. Each part has an agenda to help you get urgent needs met. Those parts have to bypass certain truths to achieve their goals. Children who grow up in dangerous circumstances become experts at bypassing their own truths. We become professional self-betrayers because we have to.

In childhood, we develop parts that keep us in fantasy, buffered from realities and emotions that feel too big to process. We have parts whose job it is to make sure all that overwhelming material gets sequestered off-site, someplace where it won't interrupt our functioning or get in the way of who we need to try to be. Our Minimizer part packages up the painful truth and pushes it away, storing it in small, tight containers in our muscles, or in our churning gut. Our Numbing part ushers in gauzy layers of dissociation or spaciness and takes us away from being present and connected to those experiences and relationships that terrify or confuse us. Our Destroyer part douses our most vulnerable, unwanted feelings in flammable acid and tries to burn them out of us entirely so they no longer exist. And of course, our Inner Critic commits us to a lifetime of self-improvement plans, lashing us from the inside for all the ways it has determined us to be at fault for the care we didn't receive. But despite all that internal agitation and efforting, the truth remains: What happened to us doesn't go away. It's still here today, with all kinds of hardworking, burdened protectors exerting their energy to try to keep it out of our awareness.

The thing your protectors don't realize is (drumroll, please; this is really the whole point of this book and of parts work and Internal Family Systems and healing)...

> ✴ There is nothing bad about you.
> ✴ You just got really hurt a while back.
> ✴ And your system developed a brilliant, albeit outdated, way of helping you survive and getting you to where you are now.
> ✴ You are innocent.
> ✴ Yes, even you.

Motherhood asks us to restore trust in ourselves. We need to know we're trustworthy to do this difficult job. We have to know what's happening inside of us and consult our own wisdom respectfully. We have to stop betraying ourselves and honor the truth.

You're beginning a new endeavor with us here—of excavating your Truths. Little by little, bit by bit, we're inviting you to try on Truths that help you peek into the recesses of your consciousness and start letting out the tender memories and wounds that your parts have been guarding all these years. When you get to those Truths, and then to the Truths underneath those Truths, you find your innocence. You witness yourself as a child: dependent, powerless, hopeful, adaptive.

You see that you did what you had to do. You became exactly who you needed to become. There's more understanding for the parts of yourself you've always hated when you behold the child you once were. Truths help start the process of rewriting your narrative with more self-compassion. And there's something empowering about speaking the Truth once it's safe to do so. You get to anchor yourself in the present and update the parts of your system who were disempowered and helpless and didn't yet know that it's safe to call it like it is.

You may decide to come up with your own Truth that really captures what your parts are needing to say or hear. But if you aren't careful, your "Truth" can easily get co-opted by your Inner Critic or other Team Kid parts and morph into a self-improvement plan or have the effect of silencing your Inner Baby. Then it's no longer a Truth. It's no longer a courageous emanation from your Inner Mom; it's an agenda-driven message rooted in fear. Here is some clarification on what makes truth-telling positive and growth-inducing:

WHAT MAKES A STATEMENT A TRUTH?

- It feels courageous.

- It validates your parts.

- It reduces shame.

- It expands your part's story and your understanding of it.

- It doesn't minimize or dismiss your parts' feelings.

Sometimes it feels like admitting the truth will ruin everything. If you say how miserable you feel, it means you're a shitty mom. If you say how scared you feel, it means you're a shitty mom who can't handle raising her kids. If you say how mad you are, it also means you're a shitty mom who doesn't deserve to be a mom or can't be trusted with her own children. It's sad but true that moms attribute just about every struggle, big or small, to their own failure or inadequacy, and Western social norms are happy to add a little gas to that fire. Many moms, especially women of color who have to navigate racist systems, feel legitimate fear about sharing their internal distress. They're worried that if they're honest about their distressing symptoms, especially with people in positions of authority, their kids will be taken away. Tragically, this sometimes happens. Women, especially women from marginalized populations, have seen and experienced nightmares like this play out through history, and they've learned to stay quiet and keep swallowing down their pain.

In some situations, it's impossible to speak the truth. That's just real. But to be healthy, moms need to be able to share honestly and safely. Moms need informed, nonpathologizing practitioners who understand maternal psychology. Moms need a paradigm shift in the world so that their many emotions and experiences are welcomed, not stigmatized. The concept of Mom Parts gives us language and new permission to describe the range and the truth of our experience without turning it into a disorder or a mental health problem.

We can move closer. We can listen. We can help our own struggling parts.

Our parts have stories they tell. They have beliefs that inform their reactions. They have hopes and fears that fuel their behavior. And they have Truths that need to be spoken. For example:

My kid really triggers my feelings of "I'm not good enough."

Speaking the Truth requires a creative negotiation between parts that need desperately to be acknowledged along with parts that have felt pressure to hide—between parts that are judged as Bad Mom parts and parts that are trying really hard to be good. So much of your good-mom behavior is sculpted around fears of being judged and shamed. There's a huge benefit to bringing out the unspeakable, taboo feelings that moms hold in secret. But if you expose a big taboo too fast or without your parts' permission, there can be internal backlash and an uprising of shaming parts who try to make sure you never do that again. In IFS, we move at the speed of trust.

The Truth Builds a Bridge

Sharing Truths connects moms to each other. When taboos are shared in safe spaces, they lose their stigma. Removing judgment and stigma is what effectively softens outer critics and creates cultural change. When moms create communities where Mom Parts are understood and welcomed, they feed and nurture a new message:

> It's not just you.
>> You aren't alone.
>> It's okay to feel all kinds of ways about your kids and about being a mom.
>> You don't have to be afraid of how you're feeling.
>> What you're feeling makes sense.
>> We got you.

That kind of shift in external messaging validates Bad Mom parts who have been suffering and in a lot of distress. As they receive the magic of supportive external validation, they relax. Their grandiosity de-escalates. They come down in volume and intensity when they feel seen and understood. That quieting of Bad Mom parts takes the edge off the hardcore Good Mom parts who were feeling really worried about you being CRAZY and MEAN. Your Good Mom parts notice that things are quieter over there in Crazytown now, and there's a settling of that wild energy that was running you in out-of-control ways. Now your Good Mom parts feel calmer and more hopeful. Maybe they won't have to work quite so hard. Maybe they don't have to hate your Bad Mom parts so much. Maybe you'll sleep a little easier tonight.

When forbidden sentiments are pulled out of the shadows, it's relieving to protector parts whose job was to manage and silence and shush and smile and perform. In the open field of the Truth, moms have an opportunity to try something entirely new: listen to their pain with compassion for themselves.

✳ Truths shift your inner dialogue from *There's something wrong with me* to *This is difficult for me.*

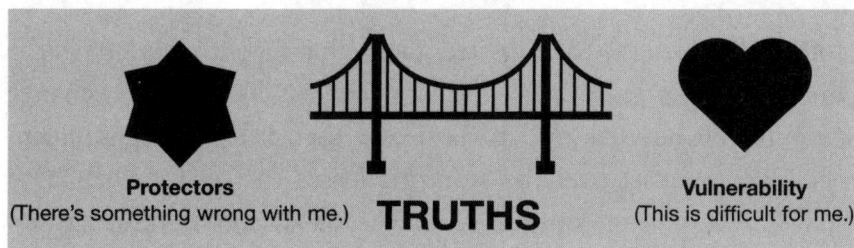

| Protectors | TRUTHS | Vulnerability |
| (There's something wrong with me.) | | (This is difficult for me.) |

We strongly suggest that you find a safe person or group with which to explore your Truths. Don't expose your Truths to folks who will judge you. Find a trustworthy person or a mothercentered space in which motherhood's Truths are understood and all your parts are welcomed.

Chapter 10

The Inescapable Vulnerabilities of Motherhood: Grief and Shame

Motherhood brings two uninvited guests that no one mentions in the parenting books: grief and shame. They move in like foreign exchange students you never agreed to host and then lay down permanent roots. There's grief over the stunning losses that come when both biology and culture conspire to make you disappear into motherhood. Shame tags along to remind you that feeling anything but pure joy about this setup makes you a monster. The grief is about a rigged game where mothers do the heavy lifting while everyone else gets to keep their lives intact. Understanding how grief and shame shape your mothering experience and learning to meet them with something other than resistance is essential to your well-being. This chapter explores why grief and shame are as much a part of motherhood as resentment and mom guilt—and how acknowledging them becomes your way back to yourself.

We expect to feel grief when someone dies. But how about grief when someone is born? Jennifer, mom to a teenage daughter, shared that when her baby was born, she felt like someone had died. "I thought there was something really wrong with me for feeling that way when I'd just given birth to this beautiful, healthy baby. No one wanted to hear me say how becoming a mom felt like an ending. But the truth is, I was sad about the life I'd lost, even though I was also really happy to be her mom." Moms believe their (completely understandable) feelings of loss and sadness are an indication that they're bad moms.

Loss is the name of the game in the early years of motherhood when so many delightful, vital, and important freedoms become inaccessible to you. Your nervous system is often out on loan, no longer available for your own deep thinking, feeling, expanding, growth, or expression. As biological hosts, primary attachment figures, and first responders to children's physical and emotional requests and demands, you use your singular nervous system as an auxiliary nervous system for these highly dependent beings, processing and interpreting nonverbal cues, feeding hungers, and soothing and regulating emotional distress. The demands on your time and energy are huge. For most moms, that registers as a loss. Because mothers have interests other than mothering(!). Let's name a few:

- art
- career
- crying
- eating and drinking (sometimes alcohol!)
- free movement
- friendship
- guilt-free alone time
- pooping alone
- reading
- sex
- silence
- sleep, sleep, sleep
- solitude
- thinking, contemplating
- traveling

Babies are, in fact, pure need and pure dependency. And mothers are very often exclusive hosts for all of that endless need. What does it mean to host a human infant?

You come when the baby cries.

You investigate all complaints.

You address discomforts with soothing.

You feed them, you change them, you feed them, you change them.

You research all possible dangers (there are so manyyyy).

You stay awake, listening, worrying.

Your body becomes a refuge, a jungle gym, a food source.

You look in their eyes, seeing intelligence and soulfulness.

You open your heart, delivering more and more energy and attention, and even a little more after that.

When we have partners, family members, friends, or hired help that can contribute to hosting the baby, moms fare better. But often, it's Mom who does the lion's share of the care work, which can occupy every hour of the day and eat through every ounce of her energy. Tending responsibly to an infant or a small child is a herculean job that affords little time for much else. Mostly it's hard, repetitive, unenjoyable work to which grief is a natural response. If you live in a culture that cannot acknowledge mothers' considerable losses, and where grieving those losses makes you a bad mom, grief has to go underground.

Grief Festers into Shame

Grief is everywhere on the motherhood path. There are losses that come when you always wanted kids and you have difficulty getting pregnant or fostering or adopting. There are losses that come when you always wanted kids and then you actually have them. There are losses when you knew motherhood wasn't your calling and yet you felt pressure to have children, and now here they are. There are losses that come when your family doesn't look like the one you imagined. There is loss when you got pregnant by accident and had to make difficult decisions that changed the course of your entire life. And there are those best-case-scenario losses that accompany watching your beloved children spread their wings and . . . fly away.

Standing at the maternal starting gates, most of us have no clue what's about to happen. We are entirely unaware that our expectations of motherhood are BS. We don't know that we're unconsciously hoping our children will fulfill our dreams and meet our as-yet-unmet emotional needs. We imagine they will fit nicely into our lives, and we can get back to being ourselves at the six-week mark, or the one-year mark, or when they're finally in school, or when they're finally able to drive themselves to dance class, or maybe, at long last, when they get married and start their own families. We lack clarity about what we're about to give up and what we're banking on receiving in exchange. We don't know how our physical bodies will feel—or how we will feel about our physical bodies—once they've been ravaged by pregnancy, birth, breastfeeding, and years of all-nighters. We have no idea that our children will, in fact, turn out to be their own unique, difficult selves who push our most sensitive buttons, because they matter more to us than anything and we've assigned ourselves responsibility for the outcome of their existence. We have no clue how excruciating it will be to watch them suffer, or to lose them completely.

We have so little control. So much responsibility and so little control the whole way through. And the grief that underlies our lack of control and our losses is a forbidden topic in mom circles, with pediatricians, and with family members. When moms speak to their losses, they're judged for it. The message becomes this: If you have parts that want anything other than motherhood, you're bad. Or you make people uncomfortable. So moms bottle up their taboo longing and their taboo grief and become . . . all bottled up. You need to know that it's perfectly normal and healthy to experience and explore your grief in motherhood.

✳ All parts are welcome, including your parts that yearn for pre-baby and nonmotherhood days. Good moms feel grief too.

When you feel responsible for the health, performance, appearance, behavior, and well-being of your dependent child, you also feel at fault when things go wrong. Moms are trained by patriarchy and egged on by biology to attribute losses and misses to our own failures and shortcomings: *There's something wrong with me, I'm not doing it right, I'm not good enough,* et cetera. In our culture of perfectionistic mothering, we know how it's supposed to look. We know how to fake it, and we know how to endure—but we don't know how to embrace or metabolize our deeply painful experiences, and we're given no support for exploring and tending to our suffering. We're left all alone to try to figure it out.

Protectors exile and silence our motherhood grief out of fear of humiliation and rejection by other mothers; partners; the medical, legal, or other establishment; and most dominant of all, our own Inner Critics. Unfortunately, it's the case that when things are difficult, or humiliating, or confusing, or disappointing, moms tend to blame themselves. Our protector parts band together to try to create a good-mom facade to battle intensifying bad-mom feelings: *I'm not a natural mother. Where's my maternal instinct? There's something wrong with me.* Moms need to know that the many inevitable losses they experience in motherhood are worthy of grieving.

When grief remains unspoken and unwitnessed, it begins to ferment into something more toxic. Without permission to acknowledge our losses, grief transforms into the belief that feeling these losses makes us defective mothers. This is where shame enters the picture—not as a separate problem but as grief's shadow when it's forced underground.

Let's Talk About Shame

A core wound for all of us, the one that drives so much of our protectors' reactions and behavior, is shame: the belief that there's something wrong with us. We are bad, not good enough, not lovable, or not worthy. Being on the receiving end of judgment or harsh commands—even the well-intended, lifesaving kind, like "Get out of the street! You're gonna get hit by a car!"—can feel shaming to a small child because children are designed to care deeply about how their caregivers perceive them. This is what keeps us "in line" and ultimately alive.

Some of us are the recipients of severely shaming criticism and abuse as children, which lays down a deep imprint of unworthiness and an abiding sense of not being welcome. Those traumatic experiences are accurately perceived by our young inner systems as survival threats. Our parts become burdened with negative beliefs, emotions, and sensations that accumulate from these injurious life experiences as well as from ancestral lines and specific group associations. *There's something wrong with me. I'm not sure exactly what it is, but I've always known it to be true. I'm not good enough. I don't belong.* This is shame, and all of us are burdened with some of it.

There's nothing quite as powerful as shame in terms of motivating conformity. Humiliation and degradation can be highly effective for keeping humans in line and creating a cohesive group that understands and abides by certain rules. While shame powerfully shapes behavior, it doesn't create the building blocks of good health. "We cannot shame ourselves or each other into a higher state of being," says Martha Sweezy, our resident IFS shame expert.[1]

Shame feels awful. If you're like everyone else, you feel allergic to it, and you do your best to steer clear of it. Unlike guilt, which is feeling bad about something you did wrong, shame is the experience of believing you *are* bad. When shame floods a part of you, it creates a system-wide experience of being fundamentally rotten—not just someone who made a mistake, but someone who IS the mistake. You feel it in your entire body: heat, contraction, and sickness that pull you into yourself, accompanied by a sense of wanting to shrink, disappear, or not exist at all.

When parts of us harbor a suspicion of our own essential badness, our systems work hard to compensate and cover it up. Knowing there's something bad about you makes you feel precarious and untrustworthy from the inside out. Shame drags fear alongside it, and that fear sets off alarms of danger: *I could be perceived as bad. I could be*

found out. I could be abandoned and rejected if my awfulness is revealed.
Fear of being abandoned or rejected drives our parts to develop compensatory strengths and strategies to protect us, all built atop a belief that we are rotten. The protection provided by our parts is truly lifesaving. It's designed to disguise our inadequacies, often by amplifying our gifts. If we can paper over our perceived rottenness with enough good (or even amazing) behavior, perhaps no one will ever see the bad stuff we're hiding deep down.

Most of us do our mothering from this compensatory place. Our Good Mom protectors silence and hold back our badness so that we can keep giving and keep being/looking good. We sweep our shameful dirt under the rug. Hidden there with all the dirt is also the truth of our innocence, our unmet needs, our grief, our tenderness, and our genuine desires. When we sweep our badness out of view, we sweep away our vitality too. Attempting to eliminate shame cuts us off from our life force, and we lose connection to ourselves.

Shame Needs Love

Shame is a marker for a place inside of you where your needs didn't get met. You had legitimate emotional and physical needs, and in lieu of getting what you required, you took on an inaccurate belief about yourself. And now you have to go back in time and do the forensics on what happened. For many years, you've been committed to believing what your shame tells you about yourself (*It's your fault; there's something wrong with you*). Those funky beliefs are deeply entrenched, and they inform all of your protector parts.

Our protectors see shame as a threatening bomb that could be set off at any time and that has the power to take down our entire world with it. They do their best to get our shame out of view and quietly, discreetly bury it. And while we forget over time the specific places our shame is buried, our protectors continue to stay highly aware that we have several shame bombs buried in the backyard, and consequently, certain parts of our psychological property are off-limits. In order to guard those areas that are off-limits, our protectors stay vigilant. They work hard to divert attention and foot traffic away from the bomb-laden spots. Caretaker parts fill up the space with thoughtful, generous gestures. *How are YOU doing? Can I get you a snack?* Superwoman parts distract attention away from those vulnerable land mines and wow onlookers with more and greater accomplishments: *Did you hear? Junior made the varsity team! And we're closing escrow on the new mansion next weekend right after I finish the Supermom Triathlon!*

As paradoxical as it seems, all of our protectors' beliefs, choices, and behaviors keep pointing to and highlighting the very shame bombs they're trying so hard to hide and forget. Your identity is constructed around NOT letting your shame be seen, inadvertently making your identity all about . . . your shame.

Since it's so fiercely guarded, shame requires courage and determination to heal. If you do some amazing, deep therapy work, you will discover precisely what we're about to tell you. And we all probably have to do our own therapy to genuinely believe this, but if it's possible to take our word for it, please do.

✳ Your shame is a mistaken belief.
✳ Underneath your beliefs and your behavior, you are innocent. You always were.

Beginning to acknowledge your shame is the hardest kind of emotional work that exists. But the benefits of softening to your shame extend beyond the boundaries of your own restored heart, into both the past and the future. As you undo the knots of badness in yourself, you reach backward through time to undo the knots you inherited from your ancestors, and you reach forward, freeing your descendants from the tangle they would otherwise inherit. Softening toward shame is at the core of all psychological healing. How can we access the parts of ourselves that are in deep pain so that we can help them?

We have to trust that it's safe.

We have to believe that our parts and their feelings are acceptable and understandable.

Really, that's what this book is aiming to do—help walk you into a clearer understanding of your internal system so that you start to grow some trust in your own magnificent functioning. As a dependent child, you had to maintain your perception of your caregivers as well-meaning and altruistic, and so you naturally located yourself as the problem. Your system defaulted to self-blame. Taking responsibility for whatever was missing in your childhood environment was the most empowering thing you could do. As long as it was your fault, you had some ability to change things. You blamed yourself so that you felt some control.

> ✴ Blaming yourself for your unmet needs as a child kept your hope alive. But it was never your fault that your needs weren't met.

When our bodies and our brains are small and young and not fully developed, our options for salvation are limited. We find the best way to forge on. We drive our shame into exile, where it largely remains, guarded by our protectors who continue to believe it's not safe to let it be seen.

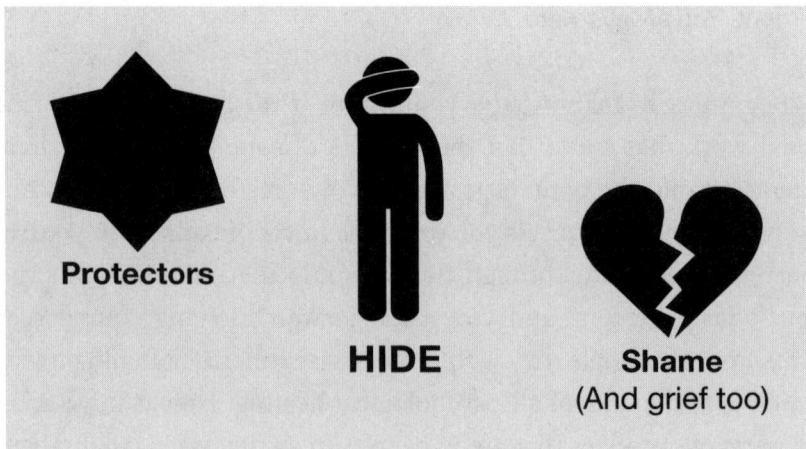

Protectors   **HIDE**   **Shame**
(And grief too)

But as adults, we are more resourced and empowered. We have the option now to help ourselves in the ways we have always needed help. We have the ability to recognize that our shame is a placeholder for unmet needs and is a marker of misunderstanding about our true innocent nature. We have the freedom to love ourselves.

Shame needs a trustworthy, nonjudgmental witness who can maintain clear awareness that even the most shameful behavior had a good or innocent intention at its core. We encourage you to find someone steady and kind who understands that parts who behave outside of integrity are still parts that deserve compassion and care. IFS therapists know how to do that. Feeling supported to be with shame and grief authentically means we don't have to bypass it or finagle our way around it. When we no longer feel the need to hide from these boogeymen, our protectors are freed up, and there is more internal space to rest and explore.

Our protector parts are designed to keep us away from vulnerability. Sometimes they need explicit direction, encouragement, and permission to step aside and allow us access to our shame so that we can listen and witness what it's holding. Slowing down is necessary to allow your tenderness to bloom inside of you. Here's a way to SLOW your system down so that you can begin to encounter your vulnerable parts:

GO SLOW

S   Soften your body.

L   Listen to what you're feeling.

O   Open your heart to what's here.

W   Wait for messages from your parts in the form of feelings, words, or sensations.

Grief Is the Place Where Shame Goes to Heal

There are times in our lives when what we really need are strategies for keeping our heads above water. Most kinds of psychotherapy are invested in just that: giving you coping tools and techniques for staying out of the depths of shame and grief, with the understanding that those areas could feel overwhelming. When we're overwhelmed, we go into protection mode, and our brains are not open to learning, healing, or growing (we can be in either protection mode or connection mode but not both, remember?). Our protectors are great at distracting and soothing and escaping, thank goodness. There are moments in our lives when we just do not have the luxury or the capacity to be with the immenseness of our shame or grief. In those times, it can be helpful to create a safe container to hold your grief or your shame until you are able to come back to it with more support. Use the tools. Take care of your parts in the best way you possibly can.

But the day may come when you do have more space to venture under all the coping and protecting, and when you do, you will discover that pretty much all roads lead to grief. Your Inner Critic, Perfectionist, and Fuck-it parts alike will all tell you over a cup of tea their painful, poignant stories of loss and unmet needs and humiliation and abandonment. If you find the courage and the compassion to stay with your parts long enough, you will likely discover your long history with loss. Making your way from protector parts to the vulnerability they guard requires encountering shame on the way to grief. But if you can get to the grief, the shame will feel lighter.

✳ Shame will lead you into grief when you stop to listen closer.

It's through being honest about shame and the grief that sits just beneath it that we heal. But we live in a world that is averse to both, with few venues suited to either. Moms don't know how to find, feel, or focus fruitfully on their grief or their shame. In fact, they're

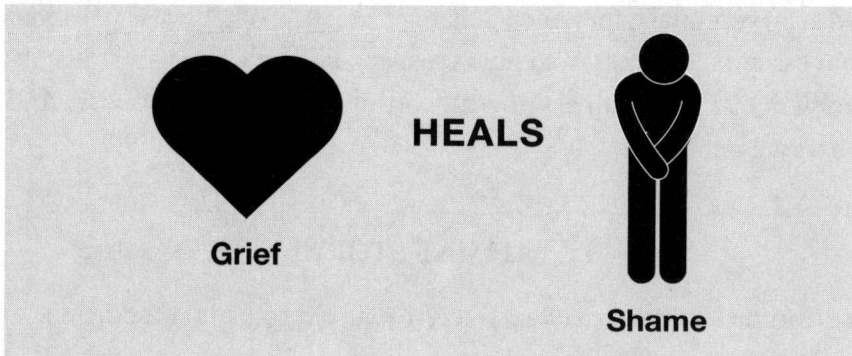

Grief   HEALS   Shame

generally encouraged not to go there at all but to instead look on the bright side, count their blessings, and all those other infuriating platitudes that people dish out to moms.

Humans and their parts don't work that way. When we get hurt, we feel it and we remember it. If we can't work through it in real time, our parts create detours and off-ramps, cordoning off entire sections of our being with yellow tape and hazard signs to help us avoid what hurts. But our minds, our bodies, and our souls need to process our hurt and make sense of our experience in order to be well.

Let's be real—shame and grief are the pits. There's a reason why our protectors devote all their energy to avoiding them. Shame and grief really, really hurt—as deeply as we can possibly feel hurt. They resonate with badness and aloneness and all that is dark and doomed. We know.

You have a thousand good reasons to keep dodging your shame and your grief. We dodge them too sometimes. But we're here together, being with the words on this page, because we want to heal. And as therapists and mothers ourselves, through our own trial and error, we've come to know for sure that you do have to feel to heal. You have to access the parts that are holding the wound in order to address and clean the wound. Francis Weller, in his book *The Wild Edge of Sorrow*, encourages us to extend a kind of hospitality to our grief, assuring us that grief is not a problem to be solved but rather "a deep encounter with an essential experience of being human."[2] When we learn about our essential goodness and how we spent a lifetime believing (mistakenly) in our own badness and unworthiness, we start to grieve. And that's a good thing.

FATIMA'S STORY

Fatima is mom to a twenty-seven-year-old son who is addicted to fentanyl and living on the streets. She came to therapy hoping to find answers that would help her get her son into recovery so that she could "save the love of my life." Initially, Fatima identified her parts as Panic, Regret, and a Mama Bear. She described many frantic, sleepless nights searching for her son in online forums and pounding the pavement downtown, searching through the tent city. She shared that her husband had written their son off after he stole a large sum of money from them, leaving her alone in her search and in her anguish. Fatima's protectors had an agenda to fight hard for her son's survival and recovery. When given the Mom Parts Truths, after a lot of deliberation, she landed on these:

> Sometimes I'm disappointed in my kid.
> Some things are out of my control.
> I did the best I could.

Fatima's Mama Bear revolted against these Truths because speaking them felt like acceptance—maybe even resignation. "Admitting I have no control and that I've done my best feels like I'm giving up!" Fatima's shoulders started shaking involuntarily, and she covered her face with both hands. Grief was here, asking for surrender. She leaned courageously into the process, and her protectors relaxed enough to let her move a little closer to her own aching heart, which nearly exploded with pain. She felt compassion for her own suffering in a way that her protectors had not previously allowed, and her entire system moved out of hypervigilance and toward calmness. From this more settled space, she was able to think about next steps with greater presence.

In the weeks that followed, Fatima's relationship with herself began to transform. Instead of the relentless self-blame that had consumed her for years, she started treating herself with the same tenderness she'd always shown her son. When her son called asking for money, she could feel her Mama Bear part activate, but now she also felt her Grief—the part that knew she couldn't save him. "I love you, and I can't give you money for drugs," she told him, her voice shaking but clear. The surrender wasn't giving up—it was finally accepting what had always been true: Her son's recovery was his to choose. For the first time in years, Fatima stopped asking, "What did I do wrong?" and started asking, "How can I take care of myself today?" She began grieving not just the son she'd lost to addiction, but the harsh way she'd been treating herself. In that grief, she discovered a new depth of compassion—one that allowed her to love her son without abandoning herself in the process.

Getting Intimate with Grief

Becoming a mom is like relocating your own vulnerable pink, slippery beating heart from the safety of your rib cage into the cold, windy, brutal landscape of the world outside of your body where all the elements can have their way with it. And you discover how little control you have over what happens to that slippery, pink heart. You come face-to-face with your inability to guarantee that little slippery muscle will listen to your words of wisdom or respect you or even *like* you. You don't have the power to ensure that little pink heart of yours will survive out there in the dog-eat-dog world or that it will call you when it promised to or come home for the holidays ever again once it's all grown up.

That externally located heart of yours makes you a candidate for incredible growth and learning. And it makes you a front-runner for considerable heartache.

Children provide trailheads for all your unmet needs and unfinished emotional business. As we've explored in earlier chapters, your protectors will attempt to get your own early needs met through your children—and they will fail. And for many of our parts, that's incredibly sad and disappointing (possibly enraging) news. Those parts were hoping for more! And they expected something different! They're mad. Or they're bummed. Or they're depressed and devastated.

They need to grieve. They need support from you to go ahead and acknowledge the depth of their feelings. Maybe you've been afraid to listen to your grief, or to be honest about how much loss, inadequacy, and impotence you've felt as a mom. If you have some courage and curiosity alive in you, that makes it easier. Community rituals and healing practitioners can all help you in accessing the remedies you need to sustain you in the dark.

Sometimes we are in so much pain that we are consumed by it. We are completely blended and submerged in our suffering and not in touch with courage or curiosity. That's how it is sometimes. We need space to let these feelings come. We need to be held. We need to feel Inner Mom energy inside us and all around us. Grief is sacred and deserves to occupy territory in our hearts and space in our lives.

There isn't much mystery in your grief. It doesn't really need to be figured out. It's here waiting for you to show up with your caring presence so it can express itself fully and be known. But your protector parts are designed to keep you out of all painful, dark, abyss-like spaces—and they hate the thought of even permitting, much less *surrendering* to, grief. Hear us out. You made it this far, and your parts deserve this. You can do it. Grief is vital. You were designed to grieve as much as you were designed to feel happiness.

Get more acquainted with how your parts are hurting and how they got here. Have a little conversation with them. It's like exchanging a few friendly words with someone you've just been introduced to. Start with thirty seconds.

Ready?

JOURNAL

Go inside and say hello to any parts that are grieving.
Let them show you where grief is hanging out in your body.
What does it feel like there? Heavy? Tight? Shaky?
Just show up for a moment and take the temperature.
Notice the environment and let yourself register more than you have before.
What does this grief feel like inside of you?

Now that you've touched your grief, notice how you're feeling toward it. Is there any new curiosity about it? Maybe you're noticing that you have a little bit more courage with your grief than you had before?

If you need to take a break here and come back later, that's completely understandable. Just go inside briefly and let your grief know that you will come back again before too long. (Placing your warm hand on your heart can feel good to grieving parts.)

And then, do come back.

And when you return to your grief, a wonderful place to pick up with it would be with more curiosity and inquiry.

JOURNAL

Go back inside and reconnect with your grief. Ask it:
What's the story you're telling about my child?

What's the story you're telling about me as a mom?
About my relationship with my child?
What are you believing about the future?

Listen to the story and find out what it is this part is really afraid of—and what it was hoping for. Can you stay present and feel its grief? Can you let your heart open to it? Sometimes it helps to write down exactly what it told you so the part feels even more seen. To begin to heal, it needs to feel your understanding and your care.

It very well may need to cry.

We can wait for you here while you get a tissue.

Take your time.

Being a mom is mind-blowing and heartwarming and soul-expanding in moments. But it's also ruthless, empty, selfless, and heartbreaking for many devoted, hardworking Mom Parts. Discovering the limits of our ability to fix things—our impotence—is excruciating. Can we have a moment for all the parts of you who feel like your heart broke a little (or a lot) since you became a mom?

(Moment of silence.)

How are your disappointed, sad, frustrated protectors feeling finally hearing some acknowledgment and validation from you?

There are times when it absolutely is true that one of you—either you or your child—will have your needs met and the other will not. And in these moments, when we accept the reality of one person's needs going unmet, grief and shame are sure to follow. When we choose ourselves over our child, requiring our kid to hold their own unmet needs, shame beckons us into its shadows. We wonder if we're selfish for leaving when they begged us to stay. We wonder if we've harmed them to help ourselves. And we question whether that's allowed in motherhood.

On the flip side, when we sacrifice our own desires or needs to meet our child's needs, we endure (another) loss. Whether we acknowledge our grief or push it away with a more forceful protector, the loss is there, as once again we are pinned beneath a nursing child, or home from work with a feverish one, declining a much-needed night out because we can't find a babysitter, maybe giving money to an adult child who isn't using it wisely—forgoing something that would be so nurturing and delicious or affirming or profitable for ourselves. We watch other people continue to engage with life at full throttle, with both arms free and a surplus of energy, and here we are once again, paused by motherhood. A still life. Held captive by maternal love, responsibility, guilt, hope, and a culture that fails to support us.

Grief is in the body, and it surfaces with a sob, with tears, with vibration and tension that rocks you in motion while it holds you in its sway. Grief is how it feels to be honest about what you lost, what you didn't get, what you cannot control, how alone you feel, and what will never be. Grief begs you to get level with the truth and to allow your heart to encounter its anguish with your entire breathing being-ness, as though you've been sucked under a giant wave with only the little bit of air you had in your lungs—and you tumble with it, flipping mercilessly, until the wave has had its way with you and lands you splayed out on hard sand with the taste of salt still in your throat. Grief is intense and primal. It knows what it needs to do. It's asking you to surrender. You can trust it. Find something, someplace, or someone secure to hold you while it thrashes through you.

Yes, it vibrates and throbs with pain, and our protectors want so badly to avoid it. But grief needs room to express itself. It's begging for you to be with it.

When our grief is given permission to pulse its existence inside of us, it restores us to humility and allows our hearts to rest and open once again. Grief cleans us from the inside out.

✳ Grief is medicine.

Chapter 11

We Have Remedies Within Us

When times get tough, we have two internal psychological resources available to us: protector parts and our Inner Mom. As you know by now, protectors are based in fear, and they help us out by using strategies of avoiding, blocking, resisting, exiling, overworking, aspiring, pleasing, and so on to guard our vulnerability. Sometimes that means our protectors do some extreme stuff. Sometimes it means our bodies feel terrible. Sometimes it means we react in ways that we later feel bad about. Sometimes it means we work way harder than we want to.

Nonetheless, every protector makes sense. Every protector has a story about heroic ways it has tried to keep your vulnerability from being harmed, usually dating back to your childhood. While times have changed dramatically since you were a kid, your protectors don't know that. They need to be updated. Otherwise, they just keep on guarding and protecting you in the same old, outdated, primitive ways they always have.

Fixers keep trying to fix.

Controllers keep wrestling for control.

Rage keeps losing its shit.

Destroyers keep harming your own soft, tender vulnerability.

So how do you relax your protectors?

It's absolutely the case that some of our go-to parts have a very hard time chilling out. It's hard for those guys to believe that it's safe to stop guarding/fighting/shutting you down. They really don't trust that you'll be okay. They've done things a certain way your whole life, and they think that's how they need to keep doing things. They're dedicated to protecting you. They care about your survival more than anything, and they're loyal to a fault. In many ways, they're your most devoted allies, and even though they may be really screwing up your relationships and your mental or physical health, it's crucial to remember that they're also heroic, and in some way, they've been your best friends.

Building relationships with your Mom Parts is a great way to help your protectors relax so that you can shift into greater calm and clarity. As soon as you begin to get acquainted with your parts, you get more authentically interested in yourself. Your beliefs and feelings and behaviors begin to make more sense to you. It's hard to hear a part's deepest hopes and fears and NOT start to feel some compassion for it. The moment you experience one of your parts as a tiny bit real or interesting or understandable, you make a leap into greater wholeness and health. You begin to make sense to yourself. There is more hope in your entire system. You might not actually be bad or broken or fucked-up.

(Moment of hopeful silence, please.)

✳ In truth, you never were bad, broken, or fucked-up. You had parts who knew how to help you the only way they could. And they may have made a bit of a mess in the process.

That's okay. It's not too late.

Getting Your Past out of Your Present

As an adult, you have power now. You might *feel* disempowered—and you may be right in some ways. Maybe you don't have enough money or good physical health or the respect from others that you deserve. Some of us are certainly more gifted with privilege by virtue of our gender, able-bodiedness, socioeconomic status, race, lack of trauma history, or other factors. But most of us are physically bigger than we were as children and have access to some money, a phone, transportation, language, and more authority from which to ask for what we need and want. We can get ourselves up and out of a room we don't want to be in, say no to things we don't like, and buy ourselves a snack when we're hungry. We can change our situation in ways we absolutely could not as children. That's power. Kids have almost no power. It's important to appreciate the profound difference that having adult power makes in a person's sense of safety.

When we feel unsafe, our protectors show up to protect us. Always. As kids, we relied on our protector parts when we felt unsafe. They were our only power, and they saved us.

Your Inner Mom is a whole different animal. It's not a part. It's not here to protect you. It's what IFS thinks of as humans' essential core nature, the spiritual center, the "seat of consciousness."[1] It's who we really are underneath our parts. It's our innate, indestructible wholeness.

And when our protectors soften and relax, we naturally move into this Inner Mom state of being, where we have access to a treasure trove of internal resources. Inside that trove, you will find empowering qualities that give you exactly what you need to be in intimate relationship with vulnerability. Your Inner Mom isn't afraid of vulnerability. She doesn't avoid it or minimize it. She knows how to be present with it.

When you sense the qualities of curiosity, compassion, connectedness, or any of the other Remedies, that's an indication that you've tapped into your Inner Mom. You've hit the energetic jackpot. There's an opportunity for healing, and this is your cue to spread the goodness throughout your system. Each of us is gifted with this reservoir of supportive energy that cannot be damaged, regardless of what has happened to us in our lives. You don't have to work to cultivate or strengthen your Inner Mom. She's always there, just behind your protectors, and she spontaneously emerges as soon as your parts chill out.

Accessing Remedies and bringing their nourishing goodness to your physical body, to your parts, and to your external family system is an empowered way to take care of yourself from the inside out. Each Remedy is powerful enough to transport you out of a blended state—from guilt into compassion, from anxiety into confidence, and from anger into connectedness. Each Remedy brings its own unique gifts for transforming us into our best selves and facilitating healing.

The Nine Remedies

See if reading descriptions of the Inner Mom's nine Remedies wakes up that specific quality in your system—and then take a moment to go inside and let the juiciness of that energy expand.

Curiosity: Curiosity is the easiest way to manually shift your state and begin unblending from parts. When you bring genuine interest to what's happening in your system, your mind and body spontaneously adjust into a more spacious state. Curiosity is the opposite of shutting down or turning away. It's the opposite of defensiveness. Being curious is being open (even just a little), which creates an immediate invitation for more of your experience to be seen and known. The moment you feel yourself become curious, you are more present to reality—to knowing yourself honestly. Curiosity is an easy starting place and a wonderful guide.

Compassion: Listening to the hopes and fears of your individual Mom Parts softens judgment and defensiveness. That softening opens you to accepting help and receiving care, which is so intimately tied to moms' mental health. A good way to begin to expand compassion is by validating your parts' good intentions or hard work (even if you don't entirely love the way your parts are impacting your life). Compassion is the heart of forgiveness, belonging, acceptance, and peace. It's an equalizer that finds love at the center of everything.

You can always offer yourself compassion. Always. Self-compassion flows between you and you and no one else. And as it turns out, self-compassion might be exactly what your parts have been needing all these years. They may not need a whole lot more. Self-compassion is a kind of wealth that no one can take away from you, and a kind of medicine that brings healing to your deepest, gnarliest wounds. And guess what: You have that power. You were born with it.

Calmness: Calmness is spacious. When your parts feel you slow down to listen, they relax and lower their voices. You breathe a bit easier and feel more at liberty to look around, taking in a bigger perspective. Things aren't so black and white, and it feels possible now for differences to coexist. Accepting and welcoming our parts takes away pressure and urgency, which allows us to truly hold space for ourselves and our children. Calmness is contagious.

Clarity: Discovering your Mom Parts' good intentions, along with their hopes and fears, eliminates confusion and restores accurate perception. Now you make sense to yourself. Accurate perception leads to self-trust. Knowing you can trust yourself gives you power and brings relief. Having clarity helps you relax and accept what is and what leads to good decision-making.

Confidence: Knowing the function and good intention of parts opens up more acceptance inside you. As you come to appreciate your parts, you can bring more of yourself to all of your relationships. You can hold boundaries firmly and lovingly, even when those boundaries are not well received. You can consult yourself around difficult decisions and rely on your own intuition and wise counsel without needing to defend yourself. Confidence breeds trust in relationships.

Connectedness: Knowing and understanding your parts creates internal harmony and an abiding sense of security. When you feel safe internally, your energy shifts from self-protection to connection and engagement with the world. From this grounded place you are more able to be present and vulnerable with the people around you. You establish a sense of home and belonging inside of you, which means you can share that belonging with your children and help them feel welcome in community and in the world.

Courage: Trusting that your parts all make sense and are well-intentioned is emboldening. When you trust yourself, you can approach your experiences (even the painful ones) with genuine curiosity and an open heart. Openness and interest create an appetite for stepping out of old patterns and into the unknown, where growth and expansion exist. Courage is the byproduct of not feeling alone—of feeling supported by your own Inner Mom. This kind of support gives you the capacity to stay present with difficult truths, and to companion yourself through grief and shame. Courage gives you strength to advocate for both your needs and your children's.

Creativity: When your system feels secure, you naturally see people and situations from multiple angles with a variety of possibilities and potentials. More energy is available to you to weave together new combinations and iterations of the life that is unfolding in front of you. Knowing that there is more than one way to do things as a parent brings permission to get curious and stay flexible in your responses. Moms and kids can grow and change, developing resilience and adaptability together. You can write a new script.

Choice: When you are in connection mode, not needing to use your energy to defend or protect yourself, you have freedom. Your vision is unobstructed, and your perspective expands to take in more of your surroundings. You experience more flexibility as you consider options you never knew you had before. Choice is the opposite of helplessness. It's the gift of adulthood and the apex of empowered presence.

LISA'S STORY

Lisa moved to the US in her early twenties from Russia. She speaks near-perfect English and works as a director at a tech company, earning a comfortable salary. Despite her professional success, Lisa's main struggle centers around feeling disrespected by her three teenage children. "They don't like me. They have no interest in what I say. If I say the sunset is beautiful, they tell me all the ways it isn't. They live to be in conflict with me. I feel so disrespected that I end up either yelling or shutting down completely."

Lisa straddles an uncomfortable line between generations and cultures. She grew up in a world where resources were scarce, adults were harsh and authoritarian, and survival was always uncertain. Her hardworking Perfectionist and Controller parts helped her escape that world by exiling her vulnerability and driving relentless achievement. Now, as a mother to teenagers enjoying the freedoms of upper-middle-class America, those same protector parts don't know how to adjust. Instead of recognizing her children's safety and abundance, Lisa's parts are stuck in survival mode, encountering a classic Inner Baby dynamic: wanting to do ALL the things for her children that she wishes someone had done for her.

Lisa gets blended with protectors who remember her own desperate Inner Baby. Her Controller and Perfectionist had to push beyond all limits to excel academically and earn her path to freedom, and they do the same thing to her kids now. Her children resent this relentless pressure and maintain emotional distance from her, leaving Lisa feeling disconnected and powerless. In response, her protectors double down on their authoritarian approach, creating an escalating cycle of control and resistance. She recognizes that her kids feel bullied by her protector parts and knows she needs to bring more heart and vulnerability to create deeper connections.

Lisa chooses these Truths:

Nothing's perfect.
Sometimes my kid hurts my feelings.

"The prospect of being vulnerable is terrifying," Lisa shares. "I don't want my kids to see me as messy or broken. I refuse to expose them to the ugliness of my childhood. I will never let my kids feel the way I felt growing up." Lisa's protectors know only one way to manage her Inner Baby's pain: strict adherence to a high-achieving, no-vulnerability policy.

As Lisa began exploring her parts with more curiosity, something shifted. She discovered how her parents used shame as motivation and how it left deep scars. Growing more comfortable with her inner landscape, she became increasingly courageous and creative in her mothering, forging a completely new path that no one in her family line had ever explored. She started experimenting with trusting her children's innate health and relaxing her control. Her growing curiosity about her own Inner Baby helped her develop genuine interest in her kids as their own unique, imperfect beings.

Six months later, when her daughter brought home a C+ in math, Lisa felt her familiar alarm rising. But instead of her Controller and Perfectionist launching into action, she paused and got curious: *What is my Inner Baby afraid of right now?* The answer came immediately: *My daughter won't survive without perfect grades. She'll end up powerless and abused.* Lisa recognized this ancient fear and spoke to her Scared part: *I know you're terrified, but that was a different world. We're not there anymore. She's growing up in a completely different reality.* As her Scared part absorbed this update about past versus present, Lisa's alarm settled. From this calm, connected place, she said to her daughter, "That must have been disappointing. Tell me what's happening in math." Her daughter, surprised by the gentle response, opened up about struggling with the teacher's pace.

Two Ways to Travel: Manually or Spontaneously

As adults, even the least empowered of us have the option to be generous with self-compassion. You can load the self-love on as thick as you desire. You can become devoted to creating and maintaining an atmosphere of acceptance and care inside yourself, and no one can stop you. But obviously life as a mom gets chaotic and complicated, and it's not always easy to find a feeling of compassion inside yourself. What can you do when you know intellectually that you want to be kind to yourself, but you're feeling distraught and distressed, and your parts are starting to freak out?

You can use a sort of "manual" approach to accessing self-compassion and other Remedies by deliberately prompting yourself to get curious about your system. You do have to slow down a bit to shift curiosity into gear. You can't just make a decision to be curious and kick your Inner Mom into action. Remember, this Mom Parts stuff is all about relationships, and that means you need to devote some time and energy to relating with your parts in an ongoing fashion. Curiosity is the easiest entry point, and slowing down and going inside is how you get there. The final chapter of this book includes a collection of nudges, reminders, and exercises for slowing down, getting curious, and finding ways to help parts soften, which—BOOM—releases compassion and other Remedies into your system.

Sometimes you will notice yourself naturally happening into one of the nine Remedies just because you're having a good day or feeling in a flow. When one of the Remedies is spontaneously bubbling up in your system, take advantage of that gift to focus on what's already here inside you—and deepen it, expand it, and let yourself embrace it fully. Any chance you have to pause and bring a healing Remedy to your parts is a golden moment. Remedies are transformative. They improve your health and update your system, creating another opportunity to get your past out of your present.

Giving Your Tired Parts an Update

Bringing Remedies to parts of yourself who are suffering, stuck in the past, isolated, and reverberating with decades-old powerlessness is the deepest kind of healing. To heal this way, you have to be in connection with the hurting parts, you have to know and feel their experience, and you need to have something new and nurturing to offer them. Now when you visit that old pain and reexperience the suffering of those parts, it's not just a traumatic repetition. It's a new experience of bringing something supportive into a space where a part was frozen and stuck in an outdated pattern where the same shit was replaying over and over.

You can help yourself now.

Give your parts the care they never got. Mother them. Don't try to fix them or change them. Behold them and hold them. Listen. Open your heart and let them feel your presence and steadiness. Bring them into your present-day life, where there are so many more resources and more love, maybe more peace, certainly more power and choice.

There is so much you cannot change. But your parts are no longer alone with their suffering. You're here now.

Chapter 12

When Good Moms Need Help

Nudges, Reminders, and Exercises

Every good mom feels bad sometimes. Every good mom has moments of failure, collapse, explosion, and despair. You can be a good mom and be struggling. You can be a fantastic mom who falls apart sometimes. Being a good mom isn't predicated on delivering a perfect performance. The substance of your heart is so much of what matters, and your desire to understand more and try again is worth everything. Shout-out to all you *bad* moms out there who feel like you've royally screwed up and there's no way to redeem yourselves. We hate to break it to you, but if you're reading this book, you can't be all that bad of a mom. You may have some savage and ferocious parts, but you also have an impulse to heal and to be a good mom. That's a big deal. We all need support in our difficult moments; we need to know we aren't alone, and we need some scaffolding to hang on to when we feel like we're dangling dangerously close to the edge.

The primary message of this book is very simple and also completely life-changing: It's normal to have all kinds of parts. Once you understand and accept yourself as full of parts that are all trying to help you, you will have changed your way of being in the world, and you've upped your game as a mom. The way you look at yourself and your kids will be more open and accepting, more flexible and resilient. That's huge. But if you want to take it one step further and discover how to specifically apply this new knowledge, especially in times when you're struggling, this next chunk of the book is for you. This final chapter is your go-to guide for helping yourself get out of the ruts and the repetitive loops you get stuck in. Here you will find nudges, reminders, and exercises to help you reconnect with your Inner Mom, unblend from your parts, and give those parts some much-needed care when they're feeling BAD.

We begin with the "Mapping-Your-Mom-Parts Worksheet," "The Mom-Parts Method," "Writing a Letter from Your Inner Mom," and "When You Have Polarized Mom Parts: The Conference Table"— four beautiful ways to get to know your parts better and deepen your relationships with them. These exercises require a bit of time and thought.

Sometimes when the shit is actively hitting the fan, we need some quick ways to feel better. We need some guidance about how to reconnect with our confidence. We need reassurance that we're doing okay or a reminder that there's a way to recover from the not-okayness of a particular moment. Experiment with these reminders and nudges and see if you're able to find your parts, unblend from them, and settle into a little more compassion or connectedness as a result. We are sending you our love and appreciation on the journey ahead.

Mapping-Your-Mom-Parts Worksheet

For this exercise, refer to the Mom Parts and Mom Parts Truths boxes on pages 203 and 204. Pick one of your Mom Parts that you identify as a *Good Mom part* and answer the following questions:

This part is called _____.
This part's fear is _____.
By doing its job, this part's hope for me is _____.

This part's belief about me is _____.
The Truth that feels validating to this part is _____.
This part is protecting me from feeling (circle one) SHAME or
    GRIEF.
This part needs this Remedy the most: _____.

Pick one of your Mom Parts that you identify as a *Bad Mom part* and answer the following questions:

This part is called _____.
This part's fear is _____.
By doing its job, this part's hope for me is _____.
This part's belief about me is _____.
The Truth that feels validating to this part is _____.
This part is protecting me from feeling (circle one) SHAME or
    GRIEF.
This part needs this Remedy the most: _____.

Pick one of your Inner Baby parts (Sad, Scared, or Wanting) and answer the following questions:

This part is called _____.
This part's fear is _____.
This part's hope is _____.
This part's belief about me is _____.
The Truth that feels validating to this part is _____.
This part needs this Remedy the most: _____.

The Mom Parts Method

Use the Mom Parts method to get to know your parts, to unblend from them, to access care from your Inner Mom, and to increase self-compassion. You can do this in a group or solo. You'll need your journal and something to write with.

Step 1: Meditation—Finding Your Mom Parts

Go inside and bring to mind a situation you want to explore from when you were mothering or on your journey to motherhood. Choose a time when you felt stirred up, triggered, or unsettled. Don't choose the most traumatizing moment unless you're already familiar with it and confident in your ability to bring a lot of compassion to it. Start out by picking a time when you felt uncomfortable in a more familiar way.

As you land on a memory or event, think back to where you were, who was there, and what was happening. Let yourself feel what concerned you, what you didn't like, or what you were hoping for.

Recall what was going on inside you at that moment. What's the first reaction that comes up? What *parts* of you react to that situation? Often there's a very prominent first reaction (frustration, worry, some inner criticism, etc.). Make note of that first reaction and scan inside yourself to notice more about how you experience it.

Sometimes there's a *physical* response like tensing, restlessness, racing heart, or stomach pain. Sometimes there's an *emotion* that surfaces with it, like sadness, fear, or anger. Notice that too. Maybe you're *seeing* something visual, something colorful—notice that. Our parts have stories they tell about us. What story is your part telling about you? What's it saying about the kind of mom you are and the kind of kid you have? What's it saying about your relationship? Start to hear this as the story of this particular part of you. It doesn't represent all of you. Just one part.

Now see if you can separate from that part a little bit. If you're picturing it, see if it's possible to get another couple of inches between you. Here's one way to do this: As you're breathing, see if you can breathe it outside of you a tiny bit. You're not trying to make it go away; you're just getting a little bit of space from it so you can see it more clearly and really focus on it. And if you aren't able to get space from your part, it's no problem at all. Just notice it right where it is.

If you are able to get a little space, from this slightly more separated perspective, can you understand why this part of you feels and reacts the way it does? Probably at some level it makes sense to you, right? When you think about your past and your personal history—as well as what's happening in your life right now—does it make sense to you that a part of you would feel and behave this way? You may have different opinions or feelings about this reaction or this part of you, but right now, see if you can acknowledge its beliefs and its feelings or its intentions. Let the part know that it makes sense to you. See if it's feeling more understood or more relaxed.

Stay with it a moment longer and see if there's anything more the part wants you to understand about it. If it feels right to you, send a little appreciation to the part or parts of you who were willing to show up and be known.

Step 2: Identifying Your Mom Parts

Take a look at all the Mom Parts and write down any that emerged during the meditation.

You can group together parts that feel related and draw lines between parts that feel really polarized. Write them down on your page in whatever way best represents how they're showing up inside you.

Now, go inside. Notice how you're feeling toward your Mom Parts. What's it like to see them as parts that are trying to help you? Or as parts that hold a lot of vulnerable feelings? Go to chapter 5 and read about your most prominent Mom Parts and see how the descriptions help you flesh out a clearer understanding of them.

MOM PARTS

- ANGRY
- ANXIOUS
- BLAMER
- BORED
- CARETAKER
- CONTROLLER
- DEPRESSED
- DESTROYER
- FIXER
- FRUSTRATED

- FUCK-IT
- GUILT
- INNER CRITIC
- IRRITATED
- MAMA BEAR
- MINIMIZER
- NUMBING
- PANIC
- PERFECTIONIST

- RAGE
- REGRET
- RESENTFUL
- RESPONSIBLE
- SAD
- SCARED
- SELF-DOUBT
- SUICIDAL
- SUPERWOMAN
- WANTING

Step 3: *Telling the Truth*

Take a look at the Mom Parts Truths and read them silently to yourself. Notice which Truth your parts are *most needing to hear*—and write it down next to the parts that most feel it.

Or perhaps you have a different Truth that's not represented here. You may need to write your own. See "What Makes a Statement a Truth" on page 204 for guidance.

Go inside and notice how your Truths are affecting your Mom Parts. Are they feeling more understood and supported? Or is something else happening? Just take note.

TRUTHS

- Kids have really big feelings. (And babies cry a lot.)
- Nothing's perfect.
- Some things are out of my control.
- My child is still developing and is a work in progress. So am I.
- All kids go through painful times.
- Just because I don't like it doesn't mean there's something wrong.
- Sometimes my kid hurts my feelings.
- Sometimes I'm disappointed in my kid.
- Being a mom is really hard.
- I don't always like being a mom.
- I'm not getting my own needs met.
- I did the best I could.
- It's not fair.
- My kid really triggers my feelings of "I'm not good enough."

WHAT MAKES A STATEMENT A TRUTH?

- It feels courageous.

- It validates your parts.

- It reduces shame.

- It expands your part's story and your understanding of it.

- It doesn't minimize or dismiss your parts' feelings.

Step 4: Inescapable Vulnerabilities

If you had to choose, is it more grief or shame that your Mom Parts are feeling? Or perhaps both? Write down *grief* or *shame* next to any parts that feel it.

INESCAPABLE VULNERABILITIES

- Grief
- Shame

Go inside. How does acknowledging shame and grief affect your system?

Step 5: Choosing a Remedy

Choose the Remedies that represent the qualities your parts need to feel from you in light of what they've been holding. Maybe some of these qualities are organically emerging in you just from moving through this process. Notice them and write them down wherever they belong, near your Mom Parts and your Truths and your Inescapable Vulnerabilities.

REMEDIES

- Compassion
- Calmness
- Clarity
- Connectedness
- Courage
- Creativity
- Curiosity
- Confidence
- Choice

Go inside and send your Remedy to any part of you that needs it. See if you're able to feel the Remedy in your body and then let it get bigger so that it fills you up. Let it fill you so completely that it spills out of you and surrounds your whole body.

And you may also feel called to send the Remedy back in time, into your ancestral line—to the people who came before you, who perhaps didn't have access to this healing (your mother, your grandmother, and the ones who came before her). Let them be touched by this Remedy too. What does it feel like to have this energy alive in your body, extending behind you in time? You can also send the Remedy forward to your child(ren) and see if they too benefit from the healing you're having right now. What's it like to share it with your child(ren)? Watch it fill them up and surround them too. Notice how your whole lineage is filled with healing energy now. Take a long, slow breath, and when you feel complete, come back to the present moment.

Look at your paper and take in the narrative that's emerging. What new information and awareness do you have about your inner world?

Writing a Letter from Your Inner Mom

This exercise is designed to support one of your hardworking Mom Parts. Choose a part that you'd like to nurture or know better. To connect meaningfully with this part, before you start writing you can go inside and locate it in your body or in your emotions. You can also consult chapter 5 to help you find, focus on, and feel your part. Here are some ideas to get you started. Feel free to expand on these prompts and follow your parts wherever they lead you.

Dear (Mom Part),

Offer validation: I recognize you've been doing this job for me (or holding these big feelings for me): _____.

I know you're afraid _____ will happen if you don't show up.

I see that you're hoping to help me in this way:_____.

Offer witnessing: I also notice how (sad, scared, tired, hungry, alone, etc.) you feel.

Is there more you want to tell me about that?

Offer Inner Mom supportive statements: I want to help you relax. I want you to feel more supported. I'm here for you. You aren't alone in it anymore. I'm listening. I appreciate you.

Love, Me (your Inner Mom)

Now try reading this letter out loud. See if your Mom Part is listening. What do you notice?

When You Have Polarized Mom Parts: The Conference Table

The goal of what IFS calls a "conference table exercise" is to help your system see and recognize all the parts that are contributing to your distress, how they're all afraid (often of the same thing), and how they're all trying to help—but using different strategies.

Your Inner Mom is here to referee—or better yet, to hold space for the embattled, polarized parts inside you. There are Team Kid (Good Mom) parts here who are worried about you being a responsible mom, and there are Team *What About Mom?!* (Bad Mom) parts here who have absorbed more than their share of negative feedback. Your Inner Mom can also sense your vulnerable Inner Baby parts, who are probably feeling a little flooded, overwhelmed, and overstimulated too. Your Inner Mom can gather all your parts together and sit them down, like you would with a group of arguing children. Want to try it?

Start out by bringing to mind the situation that's troubling you or the emotions that are roiling and boiling internally. What parts are activated? See if you can identify your parts from this list:

On one side of your imaginary table, gather your Team Kid parts, and on the opposite side, seat your Team *What About Mom?!* parts, and then, at the head, put your Inner Mom, and opposite her, your Inner

TEAM KID GOOD MOM PARTS	TEAM *WHAT ABOUT MOM?!* BAD MOM PARTS
• ANXIOUS	• ANGRY
• CARETAKER	• BLAMER
• CONTROLLER	• BORED
• FIXER	• DEPRESSED
• GUILT	• DESTROYER
• INNER CRITIC	• FRUSTRATED
• MAMA BEAR	• FUCK-IT
• MINIMIZER	• IRRITATED
• PERFECTIONIST	• NUMBING
• RESPONSIBLE	• PANIC
• SELF-DOUBT	• RAGE
• SUPERWOMAN	• REGRET
	• RESENTFUL
	• SUICIDAL

INNER BABY PARTS

WANTING
SCARED
SAD

Baby parts. You can write them in the image provided or create your own in your journal.

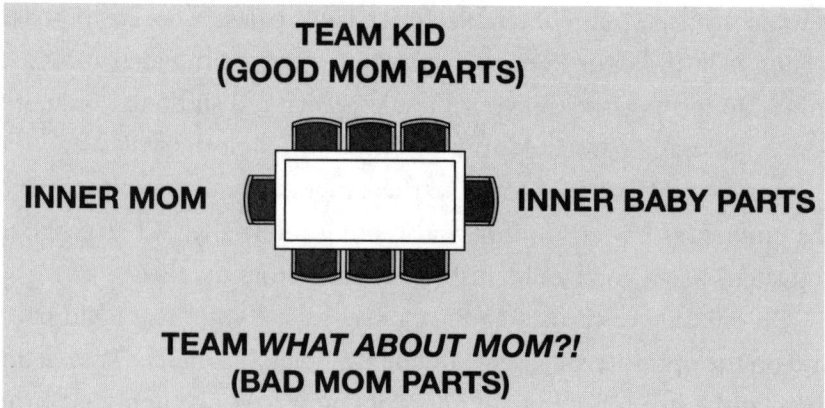

TEAM KID
(GOOD MOM PARTS)

INNER MOM   INNER BABY PARTS

TEAM *WHAT ABOUT MOM?!*
(BAD MOM PARTS)

Let your parts know they will all have a chance to speak. When one part's talking, the other parts need to stay quiet (just for a minute—they'll get their chance too), and your Inner Mom can listen to each part with an open heart and with real curiosity. Each team can choose one representative to speak on behalf of the group if that feels more efficient. Sometimes it helps to write down the names of your parts so you can really focus on them—for example, on your Team Kid, there might be a Caretaker and Self-doubt, and on your Team *What About Mom?!*, you might include Rage and Numbing parts. Don't forget your Inner Baby parts: Sad, Scared, and Wanting. Consult the list of Mom Parts for your reference.

JOURNAL

Conference table questions for your Team Kid parts:
   What do you think I'm doing so badly? What do you wish I would do better?
   What are you hoping you can change about me?
   (Write down what they tell you.)
   And next…
   Questions for your Team *What About Mom?!* parts:
   How are you trying to help me?
   What are you afraid would happen if you didn't show up and take over the way you do?
   In what ways do you feel misunderstood?
   (Write down what they tell you.)
   Now give your Inner Baby parts the mic:
   What's happening in you as we start to unpack all these hopes and fears?
   How can I help you feel better?
   What do you need from me? Do you want to come sit in my lap?

If you've made space to really listen to each side's hopes and fears, there will probably be a growing sense of calm inside you. Maybe a little more compassion. A little less urgency. More spaciousness. More tenderness for what your Inner Baby parts have been trying to hold. When we slow down and listen, it opens up the deadlock. We feel less blended with our parts, and we sense ourselves to be larger than any particular feeling or concern that's present. We make more sense to ourselves. We have more capacity to care and to respond with integrity.

When Your Bad Mom Parts Take Over

If you just said or did something you feel terrible about, here's what you need to remember: Those Bad Mom parts of you that just exploded or misbehaved or did damage acted that way because they were trying to help you. They had good intentions deep down.

JOURNAL

Ask your Bad Mom parts the following: What were you afraid would happen to me if you hadn't jumped in? What were you hoping to get for me?

Remember: Listening with care is not the same as agreeing. See if your Bad Mom parts are feeling heard. Are they feeling more understood?

Let your Bad Mom parts know you understand why they did what they did (if you do). Validate them. This is not the same as condoning their behavior. It's about supporting your parts in a moment when they felt completely unsupported. You can do that now because you're an adult. You know what those parts need, and you can mother them.

See if your Bad Mom parts are feeling a little more relaxed.

PS: You can do this for your real-life kids too, and they will feel seen and heard and respected in powerful ways.

When You're at Your Breaking Point

You are an animal who has a nervous system. That means you have involuntary reactions to stimuli at times. It means you have limits. It means you like some things and you don't like other things. It has nothing to do with goodness or badness. Period.

Your Good Mom parts need breaks. They need time off. If you don't give it to them, they will break down and burn out. It won't be graceful, and it will make you feel some shame. It's better to set up frequent, generous breaks for your system ahead of time. Sometimes our parts need explicit direction, encouragement, and permission to release. Slowing down is necessary to allow your tenderness to bloom inside of you. Here's a way to SLOW your system down so that you can shift out of reactivity.

GO SLOW

S   Soften your body.

L   Listen to what you're feeling.

O   Open your heart to what's here.

W   Wait for messages from your parts in the form of feelings, words, or sensations.

What helps your Good Mom parts relax? Here's a list of choices to inspire you. Add to it generously:

1. Being in nature
2. Music
3. Dancing or exercising
4. Time alone
5. Meaningful conversations where you can speak your truth
6. Writing
7. Drawing
8. Quiet
9. Shows, books, or games that help you decompress
10. Videos or content that regulate your nervous system

Sometimes your parts need intervention from you—their Inner Mom. Pause for just a moment and remind yourself of this: *I have parts. My parts must be struggling right now. Let me see which parts are activated...*

Remember—your Inner Baby needs a mother. If you don't give her the TLC she's craving, your Bad Mom parts will rob your Good Mom parts to try to get a little bit of relief. They'll take what you're needing, even if they have to steal it. It won't be easy on anyone, and you will feel some weighty shame. It's better to start loving on your Inner Baby a little every day. And to look for her when you feel yourself reaching a breaking point.

JOURNAL

What helps your Inner Baby feel safe? How can you let her know YOU are here for her now? (Use the aforementioned list again.)

When You Feel Like a Failure

Failure is a default feeling moms experience when they need more support and care. Yes, that's right. You're calling yourself a failure when, in fact, you're deficient in the RECEIVING-support-and-care department. See if you can chat with the harsh Inner Critic who's calling you names and let her know that we (the experts!) said that you're totally normal. You're an animal with limits and preferences. That's all. There's nothing wrong with you—you just need more care and more breaks.

If there is no extra care coming, and no breaks are in sight, and you're losing your shit, repeat after us:

I'm still a good mom.

I'm overwhelmed. I hit my breaking point because I've been momming too hard. I need more support than I'm getting. That's a reflection of a crappy, unsupportive world, not a reflection of my own goodness. I have my own Inner Baby who isn't getting her needs met. I make sense. (This is self-compassion, and you're starting to get the hang of it. It takes practice.)

When You Need to Untangle from Your Kid

How can you tell if your underlying agenda with your kid is being driven by your own unmet needs? Here are some simple questions to explore:

JOURNAL

When I'm feeling some anxiety or pressure in mothering, what part of me is most prominent as I interact with my child?

How is this part trying to help me? What's it hoping for?

What is this part afraid would happen if it didn't show up right now? What scares it most?

What happens when I interact with my child, leading from this part of me?

This sequence of questions can clarify the driving force behind your parenting approach in any given moment. Once you know which part of you is currently driving your mothering, the next, **most** important step is to bring in some fresh curiosity for that part. Here's how it might go:

JOURNAL

How long has this part of me been around?

What's my earliest memory of this part trying to help out?

Can the part feel my interest and compassion? (Check and see.)

Now, send the part some care. If the part is trying to protect you or help you in some way, send it some thanks for how it's been on your side all this time, doing its best to help get you through tough moments. Let it know you've got more choices now. And almost like a prayer, send it a blessing or a good wish or a little bit of TLC. If it's an Inner Baby part, aching with sadness or fear or longing, slow down and be its mom for a few minutes. This is when you bust out some of your magic mom moves and hold it, rock it, bounce it, or offer it whatever care and soothing worked well for your real-life little ones. You have so much experience and confidence to draw on that you can now direct toward your own vulnerable parts. This is mothering, and it's very much what your parts are needing.

When Grief Asks You to Surrender

It's helpful to start here:

GO SLOW

S   Soften your body.

L   Listen to what you're feeling.

O   Open your heart to what's here.

W   Wait for messages from your parts in the form of feelings, words, or sensations.

You may need this reminder: Grief is trustworthy, and it knows what it needs to do. It's important to your health that you allow yourself time and space to grieve.

How do you surrender to grief?

You have to feel safe enough to slow down and go inside. Then you have to slow down enough to locate your pain. Once you locate it, you have to have enough courage to feel it. You need to feel connected to something greater than yourself.

And when you surrender, who is doing the surrendering?

Your protectors are surrendering. Surrendering involves letting go of all their efforts to keep you from feeling what hurts. They stop resisting and just let the feelings come.

What are you surrendering to?

You're surrendering to something real and true: impermanence. You're surrendering to your own inner process that wants to carry you away from control and into the arms of your Inner Mom.

What makes it safe to surrender?

If you have faith, this is a wonderful place for your faith to come in. Lean the weight of your grief into any sense you have of being held by something greater than yourself.

If you don't have spiritual faith, you can have faith in the reliability of your internal system and in the existence of your own Inner Mom. When your protectors relax, your Inner Mom shows up immediately. You become more present and well resourced. What can help your protectors relax? Choosing the right setting is important. Rituals and community help. Grief is medicine. You are designed for this.

When You Need to Unblend from a Part

Take a deep, deliberate breath. This is a breath only for you—no one else. As you take in this sip of air, focus on noticing yourself, tuning out the noise and the needs of everyone else. This breath belongs to you and you alone.

By taking that breath, you buy your nervous system some time to calm down a smidge, which it will do naturally. This is about intentionally focusing on tending to yourself. You're connecting with your unmet needs, your Inner Baby, or any other parts of you that need some care, and bringing your attention to that part, away from everyone else.

- Notice the part of you that's activated; notice where it is—in or around your body.
- Welcome this part of you. Remember that all parts have good intentions and are trying to help you. All parts are welcome.
- Invite the part to take up residence in an object. Choose a rock or a stuffed animal or a knickknack and let it become your part. Listen to its story.

- ○ What is it afraid of?
- ○ What is it hoping for?
- ○ What does it think would happen if it didn't do what it's doing right now?
- Validate your part. Let it know you heard it and that it makes sense to you (if that's true; don't lie). Repeat back what you heard about its intentions and its perspective. Consult "Meet Your Mom Parts" in chapter 5 to help flesh out what this part of you might be feeling or believing. How does it respond? How's it feeling now?
- Later tonight, or first thing tomorrow morning, go back to the part and check in. How is it doing now?

When You Need a Quick Remedy

Go inside and find out which part of you is most activated right now. Start here:

GO SLOW

S Soften your body.

L Listen to what you're feeling.

O Open your heart to what's here.

W Wait for messages from your parts in the form of feelings, words, or sensations.

Ask your part which of the Remedies it's most needing from you.

REMEDIES

- Compassion
- Calmness
- Clarity
- Connectedness
- Courage
- Creativity
- Curiosity
- Confidence
- Choice

JOURNAL

What would change if you had this Remedy flowing freely inside of you now?

How would things be different? *Notice if you're feeling the Remedy a little bit now.*

Bring your attention to any areas of your body or heart that are needing to feel that healing quality. Send the Remedy there, into your bones, your bloodstream, and your organs.

See if you can get that feeling to expand. Pay attention to its temperature, its texture, and how it changes your physiology. What's happening in your body?

Invite your part to come closer to this feeling and let it see and feel how things are a little bit calmer or clearer in you now.

If the Remedy is palpable in you, notice where in your body it's most needed. Are there organs or cells that especially crave care and nurturance? Send your Remedy to those areas and see what happens when it arrives.

Maybe the Remedy is big enough to spill out of you and reach your child too. Let that beautiful confidence, creativity, calm, or compassion permeate the space all around you and your child so that it's holding both of you now.

How does it feel to be held and supported by something greater?

When There's More Than One Truth

Speaking the truth feels validating to your protectors. Acknowledging reality might have been impossible in the past, but now that you've learned a bit more about your protectors and helped them feel your Inner Mom here as a supportive presence, you've got more courage onboard to tell your story.

Make a list of your Good Mom parts and a list of your Bad Mom parts. You can consult the list in chapter 5 or go freestyle and name your own parts. One of the most meaningful aspects of this exercise is noticing which parts your system has decided are Good Mom parts and which parts it's IDing as Bad Mom parts.

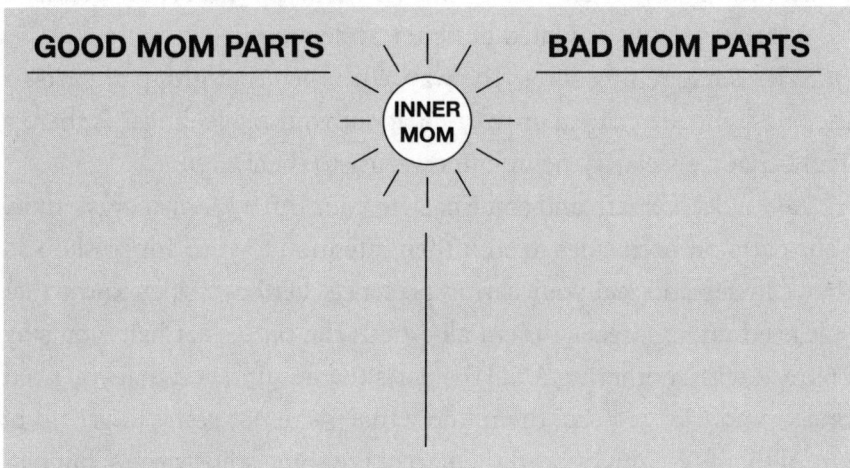

GOOD MOM PARTS	INNER MOM	BAD MOM PARTS

Next, take a look at these Truths and write down the ones your protectors are most needing to hear. Each team of parts probably has different Truths. Write the Truths next to the parts that most resonate with them.

- Kids have really big feelings. (And babies cry a lot.)
- Nothing's perfect.
- Some things are out of my control.
- My child is still developing and is a work in progress. So am I.
- All kids go through painful times.
- Just because I don't like it doesn't mean there's something wrong.
- Sometimes my kid hurts my feelings.
- Sometimes I'm disappointed in my kid.
- Being a mom is really hard.
- I don't always like being a mom.
- I'm not getting my own needs met.
- I did the best I could.
- It's not fair.
- My kid really triggers my feelings of "I'm not good enough."

Go inside and ask the parts of you whose behavior has been criticized (the "bad" parts) what it's like for them to try on these Truths.

Are they feeling validated or better understood?

What's happening across the way, with the other group of parts—the ones who are critical or worried about your big feelings? Is there a Truth that feels clarifying or empowering to them?

Take a deep breath and come back to your Inner Mom energy. Invite your parts on both sides to shift their attention to your Inner Mom so they can see and feel your caring presence. Let both sides know that you need and appreciate them all—both the parts that help you stay on track with mothering AND the parts that remind you that you need breaks and TLC too. Let them know that we're not going to get rid of any of them. We might need them to make some adjustments, but neither side has to go away or give up what's important to them.

Ask your parts what it would be like if they could lean on YOU—this Inner Mom—for care and support. What if they didn't have to try to fix each other?

Let them see that when they're battling each other, they leave no room for vulnerability—for the tenderness of your fear or your grief or your shame. See if there's a little more space now. If there is, this may be a good opportunity for you to explore the exercise "When Grief Asks You to Surrender" on page 215.

When You're Feeling Shame and You Need Your Inner Mom

When you're working hard to hide your flaws and to be the best version of yourself, your protector parts leave no room for your vulnerability. They're dedicated to keeping the tenderness of your fear and your shame out of the picture. But if you find yourself in a shame spiral, let's take this opportunity to help the part of you that's hurting. First, see if you can connect with your Inner Mom:

Remember or imagine a time when you felt like a really good mom. It could be a time when your child was sick or small or scared. Remember a moment when they really needed you, and you were able to be there for them.

Let that memory return to you now, and step into the feeling again, of being full of love. Full of confidence or courage. As you relive the memory, maybe you notice yourself being patient or compassionate with your child. Notice if you felt extra connected to them or to yourself. And remember back to how your caring presence impacted your child's experience. What did you see or hear from yourself that let you know you're a good mom?

As you reconnect with that memory of yourself, you are accessing your Inner Mom—the energy inside of you that can move mountains and heal heartache just by bringing her presence. Let your Inner Mom energy fill your chest, your belly, and your heart space. Place your hand on your heart or your belly and notice how your Inner Mom energy can flow out of you and can also flow back into you. It can move in both directions. This nurturing power exists inside of you as a resource that you can tap into and use, not just for your kids, but for yourself and for anyone else you choose to share it with.

When you place your hand on your heart or your belly, let yourself feel the safety that comes with being held by someone who loves you unconditionally. You can give yourself that gift now. You hold the power of forgiveness, acceptance, and approval all within this body and spirit that you travel with 24/7. Your Inner Mom is always here for you, and no one can take her away. Going forward, when you stop to touch your heart, you can know there is magic and love available to you right here, at all times.

Now let's invite the part of you that feels shame into the picture. Let it find a spot near your Inner Mom so it can feel her warmth and support. Bring some curiosity in. What is this vulnerable part telling you? Let it notice your Inner Mom energy here, listening with an open heart. If you're feeling some compassion, let it flow toward the vulnerable part.

What has it been afraid to feel? Can it show you?

Place your hand on your belly or heart and feel the flow of your Inner Mom energy, staying present and witnessing your part's experience. See if the part of you that holds the shame feels a bit more courage right now to step into the unknown and to share with you.

Your Inner Mom is right here, just listening and staying open. Maybe wiping tears.

Remember that your parts that feel burdened with shame need compassionate witnessing. Let this part feel your gaze and your presence here with it now. Burdened parts need to feel understood and accepted by you so that your entire system can come to an agreement that there is no longer a secret to keep or a badness to cover up. It's okay to be who you are. Some feelings just need to be felt. They don't need to be changed or fixed.

What's it like for all your protector parts to notice your Inner Mom's presence here, holding steady with your shame? They may not have known your resilience and your capacity before. Let them really absorb this experience. You are more able now to be with your vulnerable feelings without being overwhelmed. You are healing.

Acknowledgments

From Jessica:

I have eternal love and gratitude for my dad, John, and my mom, Lorilee, for starting the fire that burns in me. Eternal love and gratitude to Marc and Frank for helping keep the ember glowing through the long, cold winters. Eternal love and gratitude to Chris (my Beesh), who tends the fire so lovingly and sits with me beside it. Eternal love and gratitude to beautiful Marlo, who glows in the firelight and in whom the fire lives on.

A huge thank-you to Renée Sedliar and Michele Martin for your conviction and clarity about this book needing to exist. You made it possible. I'm so grateful to you, Dick Schwartz, for your clarity, courage, and generosity. You brought such healing to my life. To Alexa Altman for teaching me what fearless nurturing feels like. To Celanica for being here with me through it all and sharing yourselves so intimately. To Jaclyn Long and Marcella Cox for seeing my courage and capability. To Cathy Curtis, Nancy Sowell, Toni Herbine-Blank, and Toni Crossen for teaching me so much. To Kaye Namba for being my right-hand woman. To Bethany Saltman and our Bookish buddies—you cheered this book into being. To the Novembres for opening your hearts to my people and inviting us in. We love you. To Jillian Early and Rachel Brnjas for your supportive brilliance. To Emily Kerpelman and Neryvia Pillay Bell for sharing yourselves with me so I could share with the world. To Kelly Wilbur for long-term love. To my Cottles: Chris and Marda, Brandon, Fahm, and Nanus—thank you for your encouragement and kindnesses all along the way. To Austin and Margy for your joyful enthusiasm and strong cocktails. You have all contributed so meaningfully to my life and I love you.

From Rebecca:

To our agent, Michele Martin—thank you for your wisdom and for having faith in us and our vision for this work.

To our editor, Renée Sedliar, and the entire Hachette team—thank you for your steadfast encouragement, your thoughtful edits, and your overall enthusiasm and positive energy.

To Richard Schwartz—thank you for having the courage to put forth the IFS model when the world was against you. Thank you for allowing us to adapt it to fit the unique experience of moms. The world needs Self-energy more now than ever.

To our Bookish fearless leader, Bethany Saltman—thank you for seeing the potential in our work and helping us hone it. And to our Bookish peers, Christine, Patricia, Nayla, Jenn, Jess, Tracey, Lori, Sarah—thank you for the edits, the late-night talks, the collabs, the love.

To my kindhearted friend-colleagues at Second Street Collective— you make my days brighter. I'll pick up the salad.

To Adinah, Levana, and Lena—you've taught me everything I know. I hope this world evolves a little more by the time you decide to become parents. You are my most beautiful mirrors, and I love you more than you will ever know. To Rony—you make our world a better place.

To Arnnon—you make this life a joyful ride and there's no one I'd rather share it with. I love you more than words can express. To 120.

To Mom—it's an honor to watch your mothering evolve alongside mine. What a gift to be able to share that with you. I know your love is equal to your losses. Your grief is my grief.

To Dad—thank you for your calm, loving, unconditional presence always. You ground me.

To Aaron and Miriam—thank you for the long talks and for always having my back. I'm the luckiest sister in the world.

To Irit—your tenacity inspires me and I know Yosi is smiling down on us.

To my "Love Army"—you keep me whole.

To my clients—thank you for trusting me to be your companion on your healing journey.

To the therapists, psychiatrists, doulas, lactation consultants, nurse practitioners, ob-gyns, doctors, pediatricians, yoga teachers, massage therapists, acupuncturists, and other healers that are holding moms with the utmost compassion every day as they go through the biggest transformation of their lives—you are changing the world.

Notes

Introduction: You're Normal—Angry Parts and All

1. Jamie R. Daw, Colleen L. MacCallum-Bridges, and Lindsay K. Admon, "Trends and Disparities in Maternal Self-Reported Mental and Physical Health," *JAMA Internal Medicine* 185, no. 7 (2025), doi:10.1001/jamainternmed.2025.1260.
2. Milken Institute School of Public Health, "2024 Maternal Mental Health State Report Cards Released" (George Washington University, May 14, 2024), https://publichealth.gwu.edu/2024-maternal-mental-health-state-report-cards-released.
3. Allison Felker et al., eds., on behalf of MBRRACE-UK, *Saving Lives, Improving Mothers' Care Compiled Report—Lessons Learned to Inform Maternity Care from the UK and Ireland Confidential Enquiries into Maternal Deaths and Morbidity 2020–22* (National Perinatal Epidemiology Unit, University of Oxford, 2024).
4. Dana Raphael, *Being Female: Reproduction, Power, and Change* (Mouton, 1975).

Chapter 1: Good Moms Feel the Worst

1. US Surgeon General, *Parents under Pressure: The U.S. Surgeon General's Advisory on the Mental Health & Well-Being of Parents* (US Department of Health and Human Services, August 2024), www.hhs.gov/surgeongeneral/priorities/parents/index.html.
2. Richard C. Schwartz, *No Bad Parts: Healing Trauma & Restoring Wholeness with the Internal Family Systems Model* (Sounds True, 2021).

Chapter 2: Motherhood Is a Portal

1. Brené Brown, *Daring Greatly: How the Courage to Be Vulnerable Transforms the Way We Live, Love, Parent, and Lead* (Gotham Books, 2012), 10.
2. Helena Vissing, *Somatic Maternal Healing: Psychodynamic and Somatic Trauma Treatment for Perinatal Mental Health*, 1st ed. (Routledge, 2023), https://doi.org/10.4324/9781003310914.

3. Elseline Hoekzema et al., "Pregnancy Leads to Long-Lasting Changes in Human Brain Structure," *Nature Neuroscience* 20, no. 2 (2017): 287–96, https://doi.org/10.1038/nn.4458.

Chapter 3: Mothering from the Inside Out

1. Allan N. Schore, *Affect Regulation and the Origin of the Self: The Neurobiology of Emotional Development* (Routledge, 2016).

Chapter 4: Why Moms Have Mom Parts

1. IFS Institute, "The Internal Family Systems Model Outline," accessed September 19, 2025, https://ifs-institute.com/resources/articles/internal-family -systems-model-outline.

Chapter 7: There Is Nothing Wrong with You

1. Richard C. Schwartz and Martha Sweezy, *Internal Family Systems Therapy*, 2nd ed. (Guilford Press, 2019).

Chapter 9: The Healing Power of the Truth

1. Martha Sweezy, *Internal Family Systems Therapy for Shame and Guilt* (Guilford Press, 2023).

Chapter 10: The Inescapable Vulnerabilities of Motherhood: Grief and Shame

1. Martha Sweezy, *Internal Family Systems Therapy for Shame and Guilt* (Guilford Press, 2023).
2. Francis Weller, *The Wild Edge of Sorrow: Rituals of Renewal and the Sacred Work of Grief* (North Atlantic Books, 2015).

Chapter 11: We Have Remedies Within Us

1. Richard C. Schwartz and Martha Sweezy, *Internal Family Systems Therapy*, 2nd ed. (Guilford Press, 2019).

Bibliography

Brown, Brené. *Daring Greatly: How the Courage to Be Vulnerable Transforms the Way We Live, Love, Parent, and Lead.* Gotham Books, 2012.

Daw, Jamie R., Colleen L. MacCallum-Bridges, and Lindsay K. Admon. "Trends and Disparities in Maternal Self-Reported Mental and Physical Health." *JAMA Internal Medicine* 185, no. 7 (2025): doi:10.1001/jamainternmed.2025.1260.

Felker, Allison, Roshni Patel, Rohit Kotnis, Sara Kenyon, and Marian Knight, eds., on behalf of MBRRACE-UK. *Saving Lives, Improving Mothers' Care Compiled Report—Lessons Learned to Inform Maternity Care from the UK and Ireland Confidential Enquiries into Maternal Deaths and Morbidity 2020–22.* National Perinatal Epidemiology Unit, University of Oxford, 2024.

Hoekzema, Elseline, Erika Barba-Müller, Cristina Pozzobon, et al. "Pregnancy Leads to Long-Lasting Changes in Human Brain Structure." *Nature Neuroscience* 20, no. 2 (2017): 287–96. https://doi.org/10.1038/nn.4458.

Milken Institute School of Public Health. George Washington University. "2024 Maternal Mental Health State Report Cards Released." May 14, 2024. https://publichealth.gwu.edu/2024-maternal-mental-health-state-report-cards-released.

Raphael, Dana. *Being Female: Reproduction, Power, and Change.* Mouton, 1975.

Schore, Allan N. *Affect Regulation and the Origin of the Self: The Neurobiology of Emotional Development.* Routledge, 2016.

Schwartz, Richard C. *No Bad Parts: Healing Trauma & Restoring Wholeness with the Internal Family Systems Model.* Sounds True, 2021.

Schwartz, Richard C., and Martha Sweezy. *Internal Family Systems Therapy.* 2nd ed. Guilford Press, 2019.

Sweezy, Martha. *Internal Family Systems Therapy for Shame and Guilt.* Guilford Press, 2023.

US Surgeon General. *Parents under Pressure: The U.S. Surgeon General's Advisory on the Mental Health & Well-Being of Parents.* US Department of Health and Human Services, August 2024. www.hhs.gov/surgeongeneral/priorities /parents/index.html.

Vissing, Helena. *Somatic Maternal Healing: Psychodynamic and Somatic Trauma Treatment for Perinatal Mental Health.* 1st ed. Routledge, 2023. https://doi.org/10.4324/9781003310914.

Weller, Francis. *The Wild Edge of Sorrow: Rituals of Renewal and the Sacred Work of Grief.* North Atlantic Books, 2015.

Resources

Internal Family Systems

- IFS Institute: https://ifs-institute.com
- Find an IFS practitioner: https://ifs-institute.com/practitioners

Maternal Mental Health

- National Maternal Mental Health Hotline: 1-833-TLC-MAMA (1-833-852-6262)
- Postpartum Support International—support groups in various languages, trainings for nontherapists, blog, podcast: https://postpartum.net/
- Substance Abuse and Mental Health Services Administration (SAMHSA): https://www.samhsa.gov

Podcasts

- *The One Inside*: https://tammysollenberger.com/podcast/
- *Mom and Mind*: https://wellmindperinatal.com/momandmind podcast
- *The Good Enough Mother Podcast*: https://drsophiebrock.com/podcast

Books

- *No Bad Parts: Healing Trauma & Restoring Wholeness with the Internal Family Systems Model* by Richard C. Schwartz
- *Matrescence: On the Metamorphosis of Pregnancy, Childbirth and Motherhood* by Lucy Jones
- *Good Inside: A Guide to Becoming the Parent You Want to Be* by Dr. Becky Kennedy

Index

RAISING READERS
Books Build Bright Futures

Thank you for reading this book and for being a reader of books in general. We are so grateful to share being part of a community of readers with you, and we hope you will join us in passing our love of books on to the next generation of readers.

Did you know that reading for enjoyment is the single biggest predictor of a child's future happiness and success?

More than family circumstances, parents' educational background, or income, reading impacts a child's future academic performance, emotional well-being, communication skills, economic security, ambition, and happiness.

Studies show that kids reading for enjoyment in the US is in rapid decline:

- In 2012, 53% of 9-year-olds read almost every day. Just 10 years later, in 2022, the number had fallen to 39%.
- In 2012, 27% of 13-year-olds read for fun daily. By 2023, that number was just 14%.

Together, we can commit to **Raising Readers** and change this trend. How?

- Read to children in your life daily.
- Model reading as a fun activity.
- Reduce screen time.
- Start a family, school, or community book club.
- Visit bookstores and libraries regularly.
- Listen to audiobooks.
- Read the book before you see the movie.
- Encourage your child to read aloud to a pet or stuffed animal.
- Give books as gifts.
- Donate books to families and communities in need.

BOB1217

Books build bright futures, and **Raising Readers** is our shared responsibility.

For more information, visit **JoinRaisingReaders.com**

Sources: National Endowment for the Arts, National Assessment of Educational Progress, WorldBookDay.com, Nielsen BookData's 2023 "Understanding the Children's Book Consumer"